☆ A BROOKLANDS ☆
'ROAD TEST' LIMITED EDITION

De Soto
1952-1960

Compiled by
R.M.Clarke

ISBN 1 85520 4495

BROOKLANDS BOOKS LTD.
P.O. BOX 146, COBHAM,
SURREY, KT11 1LG. UK

A-DESX1

Printed in Hong Kong

Brooklands Books

MOTORING

BROOKLANDS ROAD TEST SERIES

Abarth Gold Portfolio 1950-1971
AC Ace & Aceca 1953-1983
Alfa Romeo Giulietta Gold Portfolio 1954-1965
Alfa Romeo Giulia Coupés 1963-1976
Alfa Romeo Giulia Coupés Gold Port. 1963-1976
Alfa Romeo Spider 1966-1990
Alfa Romeo Spider Gold Portfolio 1966-1991
Alfa Romeo Alfasud 1972-1984
Alfa Romeo Alfetta Gold Portfolio 1972-1987
Alfa Romeo Alfetta GTV6 1980-1986
Allard Gold Portfolio 1937-1959
Alvis Gold Portfolio 1919-1967
AMX & Javelin Muscle Portfolio 1968-1974
Armstrong Siddeley Gold Portfolio 1945-1960
Aston Martin Gold Portfolio 1948-1971
Aston Martin Gold Portfolio 1972-1985
Aston Martin Gold Portfolio 1985-1995
Audi Quattro Gold Portfolio 1980-1991
Austin A30 & A35 1951-1962
Austin Healey 100 & 100/6 Gold Portfolio 1952-1959
Austin Healey 3000 Gold Portfolio 1959-1967
Austin Healey Sprite Gold Portfolio 1958-1971
BMW 6 & 8 Cyl. Cars 1935-1960 Limited Edition
BMW 1600 Collection No.1 1966-1981
BMW 2002 Gold Portfolio 1968-1976
BMW 6 Cylinder Coupés & Saloons Gold P. 1969-1976
BMW 316, 318, 320 (4 cyl.) Gold Port. 1975-1990
BMW 320, 323, 325 (6 cyl.) Gold Port. 1977-1990
BMW M Series Gold Portfolio 1976-1997
BMW 5 Series Gold Portfolio 1981-1987
BMW 6 Series Gold Portfolio 1976-1989
Bricklin Gold Portfolio 1974-1975
Bristol Cars Gold Portfolio 1946-1992
Buick Automobiles 1947-1960
Buick Muscle Cars 1965-1970
Cadillac Allanté 1986-1993
Cadillac Automobiles 1949-1959
Cadillac Automobiles 1960-1969
Checker Limited Edition
Chevrolet 1955-1957
Impala & SS Muscle Portfolio 1958-1972
Corvair Performance Portfolio 1959-1969
El Camino & SS Muscle Portfolio 1959-1987
Chevy II & Nova SS Muscle Portfolio 1962-1974
Chevelle & SS Muscle Portfolio 1964-1972
Caprice 1965-1976 Limited Edition
Chevrolet Muscle Cars 1966-1971
Chevy Blazer 1969-1981
Camaro Muscle Portfolio 1967-1973
Chevrolet Camaro & Z-28 1973-1981
High Performance Camaros 1982-1988
Chevrolet Corvette Gold Portfolio 1953-1962
Chevrolet Corvette Sting Ray Gold Port. 1963-1967
Chevrolet Corvette Gold Portfolio 1968-1977
High Performance Corvettes 1983-1989
Chrysler 300 Gold Portfolio 1955-1970
Imperial 1955-1970 Limited Edition
Valiant 1960-1962
Citroen Traction Avant Gold Portfolio 1934-1957
Citroen 2CV Gold Portfolio 1948-1989
Citroen DS & ID 1955-1975
Citroen DS & ID Gold Portfolio 1955-1975
Citroen SM 1970-1975
Cobras & Replicas 1962-1983
Shelby Cobra Gold Portfolio 1962-1969
Cobras & Cobra Replicas Gold Portfolio 1962-1989
Crosley & Crosley Specials Limited Edition
Cunningham Automobiles 1951-1955
Daimler SP250 Sports & V-8 250 Saloon Gold P. 1959-1969
Datsun Roadsters 1962-1971
Datsun 240Z & 260Z Gold Portfolio 1970-1978
Datsun 280Z & ZX 1975-1983
DeLorean Gold Portfolio 1977-1995
De Soto Limited Edition 1952-1960
Charger Muscle Portfolio 1966-1974
Dodge Muscle Cars 1967-1970
Dodge Viper on the Road
ERA Gold Portfolio 1934-1994
Excalibur Collection No.1 1952-1981
Facel Vega 1954-1964
Ferrari 1947-1957 Limited Edition
Ferrari 1958-1963 Limited Edition
Ferrari Dino 1965-1974
Ferrari Dino 308 & Mondial Gold Portfolio 1974-1985
Ferrari 328 348 Mondial Gold Portfolio 1986-1994
Fiat 500 Gold Portfolio 1936-1972
Fiat 600 & 850 Gold Portfolio 1955-1972
Fiat Pininfarina 124 & 2000 Spider 1968-1985
Fiat X1/9 Gold Portfolio1973-1989
Fiat Abarth Performance Portfolio 1972-1987
Ford Consul, Zephyr, Zodiac Mk. I & II 1950-1962
Ford Zephyr, Zodiac, Executive Mk. III & IV 1962-1971
Ford Cortina 1600E & GT 1967-1970
High Performance Capris Gold Portfolio 1969-1987
Capri Muscle Portfolio 1974-1987
High Performance Fiestas 1979-1991
High Performance Escorts Mk. I 1968-1974
High Performance Escorts Mk. II 1975-1980
High Performance Escorts 1980-1985
High Performance Escorts 1985-1990
High Perf. Sierras & Merkurs Gold Portfolio 1983-1990
Ford Automobiles 1949-1959
Ford Fairlane 1955-1970
Ford Ranchero 1957-1979
Edsel 1957-1960 Limited Edition
Ford Thunderbird 1955-1957
Ford Thunderbird 1958-1963
Ford GT40 Gold Portfolio 1964-1987
Ford Bronco 1966-1977
Ford Bronco 1978-1988
Goggomobil Limited Edition
Holden 1948-1962
Honda CRX 1983-1987
Hudson 1946-1957 Limited Edition
International Scout Gold Portfolio 1961-1980
Isetta Gold Portfolio 1953-1964
ISO & Bizzarrini Gold Portfolio 1962-1974
Jaguar and SS Gold Portfolio 1931-1951
Jaguar C-Type & D-Type Gold Portfolio 1951-1960
Jaguar XK120, 140, 150 Gold Portfolio 1948-1960
Jaguar Mk. VII, VIII, IX, X, 420 Gold Port. 1950-1970
Jaguar Mk. 1 & Mk. 2 Gold Portfolio 1959-1969
Jaguar E-Type Gold Portfolio 1961-1971
Jaguar E-Type V-12 1971-1975
Jaguar S-Type & 420 Limited Edition
Jaguar XJ12, XJ5.3, V12 Gold Portfolio 1972-1990
Jaguar XJ6 Series I & II Gold Portfolio 1968-1979
Jaguar XJ6 Series III Perf. Portfolio 1979-1986
Jaguar XJ6 Gold Portfolio 1986-1994
Jaguar XJS Gold Portfolio 1975-1988
Jaguar XJS Gold Portfolio 1988-1995
Jaguar XK8 Limited Edition
Jeep CJ5 & CJ6 1960-1976
Jeep CJ5 & CJ7 1976-1986
Jensen Interceptor Gold Portfolio 1966-1986
Jensen Healey 1972-1976
Kaiser - Frazer 1946-1955 Limited Edition
Lagonda Gold Portfolio 1919-1964
Lancia Aurelia & Flaminia Gold Portfolio 1950-1970
Lancia Fulvia Gold Portfolio 1963-1976
Lancia Beta Gold Portfolio 1972-1984
Lancia Delta Gold Portfolio 1979-1994
Lancia Stratos 1972-1985
Land Rover Series I 1948-1958
Land Rover Series II & IIa 1958-1971
Land Rover 90 110 Defender Gold Portfolio 1983-1994
Land Rover Discovery 1989-1994
Land Rover Story Part One 1948-1971
Lincoln Gold Portfolio 1949-1960
Lincoln Continental 1961-1969
Lincoln Continental 1969-1976
Lotus Sports Racers Gold Portfolio 1953-1965
Lotus Seven Gold Portfolio 1957-1973
Lotus Caterham Seven Gold Portfolio 1974-1995
Lotus Elan Gold Portfolio 1962-1974
Lotus Elan Collection No. 2 1963-1972
Lotus Elan & SE 1989-1992
Lotus Europa Gold Portfolio 1966-1975
Lotus Elite & Eclat 1974-1982
Lotus Turbo Esprit 1980-1986
Marcos Coupés & Spyders Gold Portfolio 1960-1997
Maserati 1965-1970
Matra 1965-1983 Limited Edition
Mazda Miata MX-5 Performance Portfolio 1989-1996
Mazda RX-7 Gold Portfolio 1978-1991
McLaren F1 Sportscar Limited Edition
Mercedes 190 & 300 SL 1954-1963
Mercedes G-Wagen 1981-1994
Mercedes S & 600 1965-1972
Mercedes S Class 1972-1979
Mercedes 230 • 250 • 280SL Gold Portfolio 1963-1971
Mercedes SLs & SLCs Gold Portfolio 1971-1989
Mercedes SLs Performance Portfolio 1989-1994
Mercury Muscle Cars 1966-1971
Messerschmitt Gold Portfolio 1954-1964
MG Gold Portfolio 1929-1939
MG TA & TC Gold Portfolio 1936-1949
MG TD & TF Gold Portfolio 1949-1955
MGA & Twin Cam Gold Portfolio 1955-1962
MG Midget Gold Portfolio 1961-1979
MGB Roadsters 1962-1980
MGB MGC & V8 Gold Portfolio 1962-1980
MGB GT 1965-1980
MGC & MGB GT V8 Limited Edition
MG Y-Type & Magnette ZA/ZB Limited Edition
Mini Gold Portfolio 1959-1969
Mini Gold Portfolio 1969-1980
Mini Gold Portfolio 1981-1997
High Performance Minis Gold Portfolio 1960-1973
Mini Cooper Gold Portfolio 1961-1971
Mini Moke Gold Portfolio 1964-1994
Morgan Three-Wheeler Gold Portfolio 1910-1952
Morgan Plus 4 & Four 4 Gold Portfolio 1936-1967
Morgan Cars Gold Portfolio 1968-1989
Morris Minor Collection No. 1 1948-1980
Shelby Mustang Muscle Portfolio 1965-1970
High Performance Mustang IIs 1974-1978
High Performance Mustangs 1982-1988
Nash & Nash-Healey 1949-1957 Limited Edition
Nash-Austin Metropolitan Gold Portfolio 1954-1962
Oldsmobile Automobiles 1955-1963
Oldsmobile Muscle Portfolio 1964-1971
Cutlass & 4-4-2 Muscle Portfolio 1964-1974
Oldsmobile Toronado 1966-1978
Opel GT Gold Portfolio 1968-1973
Opel Manta 1970-1975 Limited Edition
Packard Gold Portfolio 1946-1958
Pantera Gold Portfolio 1970-1989
Panther Gold Portfolio 1972-1990
Barracuda Muscle Portfolio 1964-1974
Pontiac Tempest & GTO 1961-1965
GTO Muscle Portfolio 1964-1974
Firebird & Trans-Am Muscle Portfolio 1967-1972
Firebird & Trans-Am Muscle Portfolio 1973-1981
High Performance Firebirds 1982-1988
Pontiac Fiero 1984-1988
Porsche 356 Gold Portfolio 1953-1965
Porsche 912 Limited Edition
Porsche 911 1965-1969
Porsche 911 1970-1972
Porsche 911 1973-1977
Porsche 911 SC & Turbo Gold Portfolio 1978-1983
Porsche 911 Carrera & Turbo Gold Port. 1984-1989
Porsche 911 Gold Portfolio 1990-1997
Porsche 924 Gold Portfolio 1975-1988
Porsche 928 Performance Portfolio 1977-1994
Porsche 944 Gold Portfolio 1981-1991
Porsche 968 Limited Edition
Range Rover Gold Portfolio 1970-1985
Range Rover Gold Portfolio 1986-1995
Reliant Scimitar 1964-1986
Renault Alpine Gold Portfolio 1958-1994
Riley Gold Portfolio 1924-1939
R.R. Silver Cloud & Bentley 'S' Series Gold P. 1955-1965
Rolls Royce Silver Shadow Gold Portfolio 1965-1980
Rolls Royce & Bentley Gold Portfolio 1980-1989
Rolls Royce & Bentley Limited Edition 1990-1997
Rover P4 1949-1959
Rover 3 & 3.5 Litre Gold Portfolio 1958-1973
Rover 2000 & 2200 1963-1977
Rover 3500 & Vitesse 1976-1986
Saab Sonett Collection No.1 1966-1974
Saab Turbo 1976-1983
Studebaker Gold Portfolio 1947-1966
Studebaker Hawks & Larks 1956-1963
Avanti 1962-1990
Sunbeam Tiger & Alpine Gold Portfolio 1959-1967
Toyota Land Cruiser Gold Portfolio 1956-1987
Toyota Land Cruiser 1988-1997
Toyota MR2 Gold Portfolio 1984-1997
Triumph Dolomite Sprint Limited Edition
Triumph TR2 & TR3 Gold Portfolio 1952-1961
Triumph TR4, TR5, TR250 1961-1968
Triumph TR6 Gold Portfolio 1969-1976
Triumph TR7 & TR8 Gold Portfolio 1975-1982
Triumph Herald 1959-1971
Triumph Vitesse 1962-1971
Triumph Spitfire Gold Portfolio 1962-1980
Triumph 2000, 2.5, 2500 1963-1977
Triumph GT6 Gold Portfolio 1966-1974
Triumph Stag Gold Portfolio 1970-1977
TVR Gold Portfolio 1959-1986
TVR Performance Portfolio 1986-1994
VW Beetle Gold Portfolio 1935-1967
VW Beetle Gold Portfolio 1968-1991
VW Beetle Collection No.1 1970-1982
VW Karmann Ghia 1955-1982
VW Bus, Camper, Van 1954-1967
VW Bus, Camper, Van 1968-1979
VW Bus, Camper, Van 1979-1989
VW Scirocco 1974-1981
VW Golf GTI 1976-1986
Volvo PV444 & PV544 1945-1965
Volvo Amazon-120 Gold Portfolio 1956-1970
Volvo 1800 Gold Portfolio 1960-1973
Volvo 140 & 160 Series Gold Portfolio 1966-1975
Westfield Limited Edition

Forty Years of Selling Volvo

BROOKLANDS ROAD & TRACK SERIES

Road & Track on Alfa Romeo 1964-1970
Road & Track on Alfa Romeo 1971-1976
Road & Track on Alfa Romeo 1977-1989
Road & Track on Aston Martin 1962-1990
R & T on Auburn Cord and Duesenburg 1952-84
Road & Track on Audi & Auto Union 1952-1980
Road & Track on Audi & Auto Union 1980-1986
Road & Track on Austin Healey 1953-1970
Road & Track on BMW Cars 1966-1974
Road & Track on BMW Cars 1975-1978
Road & Track on BMW Cars 1979-1983
R & T on Cobra, Shelby & Ford GT40 1962-1992
Road & Track on Corvette 1953-1967
Road & Track on Corvette 1968-1982
Road & Track on Corvette 1982-1986
Road & Track on Corvette 1986-1990
Road & Track on Ferrari 1975-1981
Road & Track on Ferrari 1981-1984
Road & Track on Ferrari 1984-1988
Road & Track on Fiat Sports Cars 1968-1987
Road & Track on Jaguar 1950-1960
Road & Track on Jaguar 1961-1968
Road & Track on Jaguar 1968-1974
Road & Track on Jaguar 1974-1982
Road & Track on Jaguar 1983-1989
Road & Track on Lamborghini 1964-1985
Road & Track on Lotus 1972-1983
R & T on Mazda RX-7 & MX-5 Miata 1986-1991
Road & Track on Mercedes 1952-1962
Road & Track on Mercedes 1963-1970
Road & Track on Mercedes 1971-1979
Road & Track on Mercedes 1980-1987
Road & Track on MG Sports Cars 1949-1961
Road & Track on MG Sports Cars 1962-1980
R & T on Nissan 300-ZX & Turbo 1984-1989
Road & Track on Pontiac 1960-1983
Road & Track on Porsche 1951-1967
Road & Track on Porsche 1968-1971
Road & Track on Porsche 1972-1975
Road & Track on Porsche 1975-1978
Road & Track on Porsche 1979-1982
Road & Track on Porsche 1985-1988
R & T on Rolls Royce & Bentley 1950-1965
R & T on Rolls Royce & Bentley 1966-1984
Road & Track on Saab 1972-1992
R & T on Toyota Sports & GT Cars 1966-1984
R & T on Triumph Sports Cars 1953-1967
R & T on Triumph Sports Cars 1967-1974
R & T on Triumph Sports Cars 1974-1982
Road & Track on Volkswagen 1951-1968
Road & Track on Volkswagen 1968-1978
Road & Track on Volkswagen 1978-1985
Road & Track on Volvo 1957-1974
Road & Track on Volvo 1977-1994
R & T - Henry Manney at Large & Abroad
R & T - Peter Egan's "Side Glances"
R & T - Peter Egan "At Large"

BROOKLANDS CAR AND DRIVER SERIES

Car and Driver on BMW 1955-1977
Car and Driver on Corvette 1978-1982
Car and Driver on Corvette 1983-1988
C and D on Datsun Z 1600 & 2000 1966-1984
Car and Driver on Ferrari 1955-1962
Car and Driver on Ferrari 1963-1975
Car and Driver on Ferrari 1976-1983
Car and Driver on Mopar 1956-1967
Car and Driver on Mopar 1968-1975
Car and Driver on Mustang 1964-1972
Car and Driver on Pontiac 1961-1975
Car and Driver on Porsche 1955-1962
Car and Driver on Porsche 1963-1970
Car and Driver on Porsche 1970-1976
Car and Driver on Porsche 1977-1981
Car and Driver on Porsche 1982-1986
Car and Driver on Volvo 1955-1986

RACING

Le Mans - The Jaguar Years - 1949-1957
Le Mans - The Ferrari Years - 1958-1965
Le Mans - The Ford & Matra Years - 1966-1974
Le Mans - The Porsche Years - 1975-1982

A COMPREHENSIVE GUIDE

BMW 2002

BROOKLANDS PRACTICAL CLASSICS SERIES

PC on Austin A40 Restoration
PC on Land Rover Restoration
PC on Metalworking in Restoration
PC on Midget/Sprite Restoration
PC on MGB Restoration
PC on Sunbeam Rapier Restoration
PC on Triumph Herald/Vitesse
PC on Spitfire Restoration

BROOKLANDS HOT ROD 'MUSCLECAR & HI-PO ENGINES' SERIES

Chevy 265 & 283
Chevy 302 & 327
Chevy 348 & 409
Chevy 350 & 400
Chevy 396 & 427
Chevy 454 thru 512
Chrysler Hemi
Chrysler 273, 318, 340 & 360
Chrysler 361, 383, 400, 413, 426, 440
Ford 289, 302, Boss 302 & 351W
Ford 351C & Boss 351
Ford Big Block

BROOKLANDS RESTORATION SERIES

Auto Restoration Tips & Techniques
Basic Bodywork Tips & Techniques
BMW 2002 Restoration Guide
Classic Camaro Restoration
Chevrolet High Performance Tips & Techniques
Chevy Engine Swapping Tips & Techniques
Chevy-GMC Pickup Repair
Chrysler Engine Swapping Tips & Techniques
Engine Swapping Tips & Techniques
Ford Pickup Repair
Land Rover Restoration Tips & Techniques
MG 'T' Series Restoration Guide
MGA Restoration Guide
Mustang Restoration Tips & Techniques

MOTORCYCLING

BROOKLANDS ROAD TEST SERIES

AJS & Matchless Gold Portfolio 1945-1966
BSA Singles Gold Portfolio 1945-1963
BSA Singles Gold Portfolio 1964-1974
BSA Twins A7 & A10 Gold Portfolio 1946-1962
BSA Twins A50 & A65 Gold Portfolio 1962-1973
BMW Motorcycles Gold Portfolio 1950-1971
BMW Motorcycles Gold Portfolio 1971-1976
Ducati Gold Portfolio 1960-1974
Ducati Gold Portfolio 1974-1978
Ducati Gold Portfolio 1978-1982
Laverda Gold Portfolio 1967-1977
Moto Guzzi Gold Portfolio 1949-1973
Norton Commando Gold Portfolio 1968-1977
Triumph Bonneville Gold Portfolio 1959-1983
Vincent Gold Portfolio 1945-1980

BROOKLANDS CYCLE WORLD SERIES

Cycle World on BMW 1974-1980
Cycle World on BMW 1981-1986
Cycle World on Ducati 1982-1991
Cycle World on Harley-Davidson 1962-1968
Cycle World on Harley-Davidson 1978-1983
Cycle World on Harley-Davidson 1983-1987
Cycle World on Harley-Davidson 1987-1990
Cycle World on Harley-Davidson 1990-1992
Cycle World on Honda 1962-1967
Cycle World on Honda 1968-1971
Cycle World on Honda 1971-1974
Cycle World on Husqvarna 1966-1976
Cycle World on Husqvarna 1977-1984
Cycle World on Kawasaki 1966-1971
Cycle World on Kawasaki Off-Road Bikes 1972-1979
Cycle World on Kawasaki Street Bikes 1972-1976
Cycle World on Norton 1962-1971
Cycle World on Suzuki 1962-1970
Cycle World on Suzuki Off-Road Bikes 1971-1976
Cycle World on Suzuki Street Bikes 1971-1976
Cycle World on Triumph 1967-1972
Cycle World on Yamaha 1962-1969
Cycle World on Yamaha Off-Road Bikes 1970-1974
Cycle World on Yamaha Street Bikes 1970-1974

MILITARY

BROOKLANDS MILITARY VEHICLES SERIES

Allied Military Vehicles No.2 1941-1946
Complete WW2 Military Jeep Manual
Dodge Military Vehicles No.1 1940-1945
Hail To The Jeep
Military & Civilian Amphibians 1940-1990
Off Road Jeeps: Civilian & Military 1944-1971
US Military Vehicles 1941-1945
US Army Military Vehicles WW2-TM9-2800
VW Kubelwagen Military Portfolio 1940-1990
WW2 Jeep Military Portfolio 1941-1945

20018

CONTENTS

ACKNOWLEDGEMENTS

For more than 35 years, Brooklands Books have been publishing compilations of road tests and other articles from the English speaking world's leading motoring magazines. We have already published more than 600 titles, and in these we have made available to motoring enthusiasts some 20,000 stories which would otherwise have become hard to find. For the most part, our books focus on a single model, and as such they have become an invaluable source of information. As Bill Boddy of *Motor Sport* was kind enough to write when reviewing one of our Gold Portfolio volumes, the Brooklands catalogue "must now constitute the most complete historical source of reference available, at least of the more recent makes and models."

Even so, we are constantly being asked to publish new titles on cars which have a narrower appeal than those we have already covered in our main series. The economics of book production make it impossible to cover these subjects in our main series, but Limited Edition volumes like this one give us a way to tackle these less popular but no less worthy subjects. This additional range of books is matched by a Limited Edition - Extra series, which contains volumes with further material to supplement existing titles in our Road Test and Gold Portfolio ranges.

Both the Limited Edition and Limited Edition - Extra series maintain the same high standards of presentation and reproduction set by our established ranges. However, each volume is printed in smaller quantities - which is perhaps the best reason we can think of why you should buy this book now. We would also like to remind readers that we are always open to suggestions for new titles; perhaps your club or interest group would like us to consider a book on your particular subject?

Finally, we are more than pleased to acknowledge that Brooklands Books rely on the help and co-operation of those who publish the magazines where the articles in our books originally appeared. For this present volume, we gratefully acknowledge the continued support of the publishers of *Autocar, Automobile Topics, Automobile Year Book, Car Life, Car South Africa, Cars, Cars Year Book, Fact Book of Cars, Hot Rod, Motor Life, Motor Trend, Road & Track Special, Speed Age* and *Wheels* for allowing us to include their valuable and informative copyright stories.

R.M. Clarke.

De Soto Produce a V-Eight

Although similar in chassis design and body outline to other De Soto models, the Fire Dome Eight is identified by different front wing treatment and the cool air intake for the carburettor on top of the bonnet.

THE Chrysler Corporation has just introduced a new De Soto model to be known as the Fire Dome Eight, which incorporates all the popular current design trends in the United States. It is powered by a new V-eight engine with overhead valves and is offered with the choice of two semi-automatic transmissions. Other optional equipment includes vacuum servo braking, hydraulic power-operated steering and electric window lifts.

The De Soto V-eight engine is being made in an entirely new factory of 328,000 sq ft. It is a highly mechanized factory, with nearly every moving operation carried out electrically, hydraulically or mechanically. Production capacity is one engine per minute. In general layout the engine is similar to the larger Chrysler power unit, being a 90 deg V-eight with inclined valves in hemispherical heads operated through push-rods from a single camshaft. It is, however, a smaller unit delivering 160 b.h.p. from a swept volume of 4,524 c.c., whereas the Chrysler, which has now been in production for a year, gives 180 b.h.p. from 5,425 c.c.

It is claimed that the new engine will operate satisfactorily on ordinary fuels. It has hydraulic tappets and a full-flow external oil filter. The carburettor is a Carter dual downdraught with a thermostatically operated choke and it feeds into an inlet manifold heated by exhaust gas. The carburettor body is water jacketed to discourage ice formation in extreme conditions and to improve the idling characteristics when warm. The cylinder bore is greater than the stroke, so that the mean piston speed is low, and the cylinder block is a short, rigid structure which extends down only to the centre line of the crankshaft. The short four-throw crankshaft is counterbalanced and runs in steel-backed white metal bearings.

Brakes on the Fire Dome Eight are of 12in diameter, claimed to be as large as any fitted in America, and the optional vacuum servo is said to halve the pedal effort required. The power steering is the Gemmer hydraulic type offered for the past year on Chrysler cars.

The body is upholstered in nylon with foam rubber cushions. Tinted glare-reducing safety glass is optional and two-speed electrical wipers are fitted.

Other De Soto and Dodge models continue without major changes. They are fitted with a 97 b.h.p. six-cylinder side-valve engine of 3,567 c.c., similar to that used in the Plymouth. The Dodge Kingsway Custom and Kingsway De Luxe, together with the De Soto Diplomat Custom and Diplomat De Luxe, have the same chassis as the Fire Dome Eight. The Dodge Kingsway and the De Soto Diplomat are smaller cars on a 9ft 3in wheelbase. Mechanical changes include improved dampers, stronger brake back plates and bonded brake linings, also minor improvements to the synchromesh gear boxes and rear axles.

Sales in Britain to buyers with the necessary foreign currency are handled by Chrysler Motors, Ltd., Kew Gardens, Surrey.

SPECIFICATION

Engine.—V-eight 90 deg. 92 × 84.9 mm, 4,524 c.c., o.h.v. push rods, with hemispherical heads. Compression ratio 7.1 to 1. 160 b.h.p. at 4,400 r.p.m. Max. torque 250 lb ft at 2,000 r.p.m.

Transmission.—Dry single-plate clutch and three-speed synchromesh gear box with optional overdrive. Overall ratios 3.54, 6.47, and 9.1 to 1. Reverse 12.3 to 1. Optional semi-automatic transmission with fluid coupling and gear box or torque converter and two-range gear set. Ratios : Low range 7.6, 14.43. High range, 3.73, 6.52 to 1. Reverse 14.9 to 1. Alternative axles, 3.36, 3.91, 4.1 to 1.

Suspension.—Wishbones and coil springs with anti-roll bar at front. Half-elliptic rear.

Wheels and Brakes.—Steel disc wheels, 7.60-15in tyres. Hydraulic brakes with 12in drums. Vacuum servo optional.

Dimensions.—Wheelbase 10ft 5½in. Track (front) 4ft 8⅞in, (rear) 4ft 11¾in. Length 17ft 4½in. Width 6ft 2½in. Height (unladen) 5ft 5⅜in. Weight dry 3,760 lb.

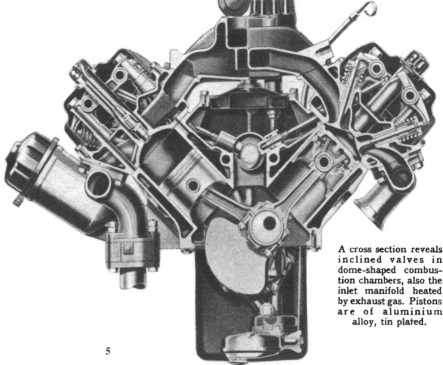

A cross section reveals inclined valves in dome-shaped combustion chambers, also the inlet manifold heated by exhaust gas. Pistons are of aluminium alloy, tin plated.

MT RESEARCH TESTS THE . . .

'52 FIREDOME DE SOTO

AFTER MILES OF TORTUOUS TESTING, THE FIREDOME DE SOTO IS JUDGED TO BE A CAR OF CONTRADICTIONS

Course includes terrain which provides severe test of handling qualities, hillclimbing ability, heating characteristics

AN ENGINE ten years ahead of the rest of the car is what MOTOR TREND Research feels to be the most important single statement that can be made about the new V-8 DeSoto. This is flattering—but only to the engine. We found that the contrast between this powerplant—one of the very best being made in the world today—and the fairly unimpressive and sometimes disappointing qualities of the balance of the car left us all with highly mixed emotions. Here's why:

"FireDome"

Such is the name of DeSoto's V-8 engine which renders with ease 160 bhp from a mere 273 cubic inches. In spite of all its parts being very lightly stressed, in spite of a "low" compression ratio of 7.1:1, it leads the entire industry (all full-sized cars) in power developed per each cubic inch of displacement, and does it

on regular grade gasoline, not premium.

FireDome is essentially a scaled-down version of FirePower, Chrysler's big V-8. Readers of MOTOR TREND are already familiar with the characteristics and virtues of this power unit ("Why The Efficiency of FirePower," MOTOR TREND, Dec. 1951 and "Chrysler Wins Engineering Award," MOTOR TREND, Feb. 1952) and to discuss this engine in detail another time is hardly reasonable. Let us sum it up this way: for well-understood engineering reasons, the most efficient and the best-performing spark-ignition, internal combustion engines in the world use laterally opposed valves in a hemispherical or dome-shaped combustion chamber. These engines are almost always made in very limited num-

BY GRIFF BORGESON

bers for a high unit price—except in the case of FireDome and FirePower. Here a manufacturer has dared to set the pace for the industry by putting into mass production what is pretty universally recognized as the ideal. It's the automotive "scoop" of the decade.

FireDome's surging delivery of power throughout the speed range is impressive and gratifying. Our test car's hydraulic tappets remained quiet at all times, which is more than can be said of some other engines so equipped. Torque is so good during hill-climbing that it's hard to believe that you're not in third gear, when you're actually in fourth. No matter how steep the hill, nor how heavily the engine was loaded, we heard no pinging, in spite of "Regular" Mobilgas being used as fuel.

All the organs of the engine that require periodic servicing are easily accessible, except for the distributor. To work on this

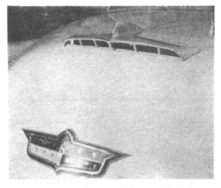

All instruments and controls are perfectly grouped for driver convenience and visibility in the FireDome DeSoto

Sole mark of significant distinction between '52 and '51 DeSotos is the functional airscoop on the '52 hood

Chair-height seats and wide-opening doors make getting in and out of the DeSoto a comfortable, easy maneuver

conveniently, you must remove the carburetor air cleaner and squat on top of the engine. In actuality, this is a very minor "inconvenience."

Power Steering

Here is another Chrysler Engineering scoop. After a couple of thousand miles of living with it, we feel that it's safe to say that if you've once owned a car with power steering you're not likely to go back to the old style. Seriously, after a day's outing in a P-S job, your standard-steering, late-model car can feel very much as though it has a flat front tire.

Imagine just 3½ turns of the steering wheel from lock to lock plus a powerful hydraulic boost and you have a startlingly quick and easy way of directing your car. In fact, if you're not perfectly adjusted to this assisted quick steering, it's not hard to get off the beam in a low speed emergency or during high speed cornering. The "feel" of power steering is hardly perceptible—it feels, from lock to lock, like "play" in normal steering.

Power steering is a super-sensitive tool and caution should be observed in learn-

ing its use. It's a blessing while parking or executing extreme low speed maneuvers with a car using large cross-section tires, and it does an immense job of reducing the fatigue that so often goes with day-long driving. But it has its price: it consumes horsepower and, therefore, fuel; it is an accessory costing $208. Is it worth the price? To some it definitely is; to others, no.

Transmission

"Ouch!" the drive train seemed to say as it buckled when we made a gentle shift from LOW range to HIGH. This was a tribute to the non-slip characteristics of the latest version of the hydraulic coupling known as Fluid Drive. It takes hold instantly in any gear—there's no slushy sound of the driving element of the non-mechanical clutch trying desperately to inspire a reaction in the driven element. In fact, the transmission of power was so sudden that one was reminded of the "all-in" or "all-out" clutches of certain high-performance machines. And one also wondered how long the driveshaft, universal

(Continued on next page)

Transmission tunnel makes huge hump in front floorboard. Metal extension below instrument panel has no function

Photos by Eric Rickman and Jack Campbell

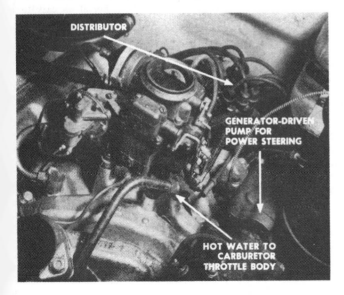

DISTRIBUTOR

GENERATOR-DRIVEN PUMP FOR POWER STEERING

HOT WATER TO CARBURETOR THROTTLE BODY

GENERATOR

POWER STEERING OIL RESERVOIR

DISTRIBUTOR

POWER TAKEOFF FOR POWER STEERING

FIRE DOME EIGHT

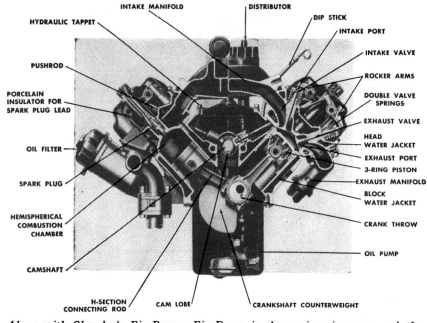

Labels around the engine cutaway:

INTAKE MANIFOLD · DISTRIBUTOR · DIP STICK · INTAKE PORT · INTAKE VALVE · ROCKER ARMS · DOUBLE VALVE SPRINGS · EXHAUST VALVE · HEAD WATER JACKET · EXHAUST PORT · 3-RING PISTON · EXHAUST MANIFOLD · BLOCK WATER JACKET · CRANK THROW · OIL PUMP

HYDRAULIC TAPPET · PUSHROD · PORCELAIN INSULATOR FOR SPARK PLUG LEAD · OIL FILTER · SPARK PLUG · HEMISPHERICAL COMBUSTION CHAMBER · CAMSHAFT · H-SECTION CONNECTING ROD · CAM LOBE · CRANKSHAFT COUNTERWEIGHT

Along with Chrysler's FirePower, FireDome is the engineering scoop of the decade, tops all its competition in power output per cubic inch of displacement

DE SOTO FIREDOME TEST TABLE

PERFORMANCE
CLAYTON CHASSIS DYNAMOMETER TEST

RPM	MPH	ROAD HP
1800	17	50
2000	39	68
3200	72 (maximum)	88

Per cent of advertised hp delivered to driving wheels—55.0

ACCELERATION TRIALS (SECONDS)
(Checked with fifth wheel and electric speedometer)

Standing start ¼ mile—3rd gear only :20.36
0-30 mph (0-29 car speedometer reading)—
Low Range—:04.69   High Range—:05.86
0-60 mph (0-63 car speedometer reading)—
Low to High—15.72   High Only :15.72
10-60 mph in fourth—Impossible to obtain, due to kickdown feature.
30-60 mph in fourth gear :12.70

TOP SPEED (MPH)
(Clocked speeds over surveyed ¼ mile)

Fastest one-way run 99.33
Average of four runs 98.14

FUEL CONSUMPTION IN MILES PER GALLON
(Mobilgas Special used throughout trip)

Steady 30 mph 19.0
Steady 45 mph 18.7
Steady 60 mph 16.5
Approximate average in traffic 14.8

BRAKE CHECK
(Checked with electrically actuated detonator)

Stopping distance at
30 mph   44 ft. ½ in.
45 mph   110 ft. 0 in.
60 mph   221 ft. 5 in.

SPEEDOMETER CHECK
(Checked with fifth wheel and electric speedometer)

ACTUAL	INDICATED	ERROR (%)
30	29	-3.3
45	47	4.4
60	63	5.0

Odometer correction factor for 100 miles .992

GENERAL SPECIFICATIONS
ENGINE

Type—90° V-8, laterally-inclined overhead valves
Bore and stroke   3⅝ x 3¹¹⁄₃₂
Stroke/bore ratio   .922:1
Compression ratio   7.1:1
Displacement   276.1 cu. in.
Advertised bhp   160 @ 4400 rpm
Piston travel @ max. bhp   2658 ft. per min.
Bhp per cu. in.   .5795
Maximum torque   250 lbs. ft. @ 2000 rpm

DRIVE SYSTEM

Transmission:
Automatic—Fluid coupling with gears. Ratios:

Low Range—First—3.87   Second—2:04
High Range—Third—1.75   Fourth—1.00
                    Reverse—3.99
Conventional—Synchro mesh with single dry plate clutch. Ratios:
First—2.57   Second—1.83
Third—1.00   Reverse—3.48
          Optional overdrive available.
Rear Axle:
Exposed drive shaft, semi-floating axle, hypoid bevel gears. Ratios:
Automatic transmission—3.73, 3.91 optional
Conventional transmission—3.73, 3.54 optional
Conventional with OD-4.1, 3.36 optional

DIMENSIONS

Wheelbase   125.5 in.
Tread   Front—56⁵⁄₁₆ in.; Rear—59³⁄₁₆ in.
Wheelbase/tread ratio   2.17:1
Overall width   74⅛ in.
Overall length   208⅜ in.
Overall height, unloaded   65⅝ in.
Turning radius   20 ft., 2 in.
Turns, lock to lock   3½
Steering ratio—power   16.2:1
Steering ratio—conventional   22.2:1
Weight (test car)   4090 lbs.
Weight/bhp ratio   25.6:1
Weight/road hp ratio   46.5:1
Weight distribution (front to rear)   57.2/42.8

INTERIOR SAFETY CHECK CHART

QUESTION	YES	NO
1. Blind spot at left windshield post at a minimum?	X	
2. Vision to right rear satisfactory?	X	
3. Positive lock to prevent doors from being opened from inside?		X
4. Does adjustable front seat lock securely in place?	X	
5. Minimum of projections on dashboard face?		X
6. Is emergency brake an emergency brake and is it accessible to both driver and passenger?		X
7. Are cigarette lighter and ash tray both located conveniently for driver?		X
8. Is rear vision mirror positioned so as not to cause blind spot for driver?	X	
TOTAL FOR DE SOTO		62.5

OPERATING COST PER MILE ANALYSIS

1. Cost of gasoline   136.25
2. Cost of insurance   136.50
3. First year's depreciation   293.00
4. Maintenance:
   A. Two new tires   56.24
   B. Brake reline   18.95
   C. Major tune-up   8.50
   D. Renew front fender   58.00
   E. Renew rear bumper   35.20
   F. Adjust automatic transmission—change lubricant   1.75
First year cost of operation in cents per mile   7.4c

—MT Research Staff

joints, differential, and axles would take the pounding. They took it, but it was rough.

As our test car was set up, we found that the LOW range was virtually useless for any really meaningful acceleration. You'd step on it in first gear and the engine would peak out—would have gone as fast as it could—within a few seconds. To get into second you had to take your foot all the way off the throttle and wait a *very* long time for the shifting mechanism to put you into second gear, thereby losing any advantage gained from the lightning responsiveness of the FireDome engine.

At any rate, you got into second gear, wound the engine up again, and shifted to the HIGH range. The DeSoto clutch has a huge assist spring which, on our test car, was probably out of adjustment. The result was that, shifting to HIGH, removing foot from clutch and hitting the throttle simultaneously, the clutch pedal stayed on the floorboard of its own accord! Naturally, the engine screamed in protest and nothing happened. You let off on the throttle, things slowed down a bit and all of a sudden, "SNAP!" . . . the clutch flipped out automatically, the drive train protested audibly, and power hit the driving wheels without warning. Now you were in third gear, but getting there wasn't easy.

We all agreed that some sort of signal, telling you when you were in third or fourth, would be an asset on the DeSoto.

Firedome engine has a rugged and compact crankshaft and piston assembly

These gears have much the same "feel" when engaged and it's not at all easy to tell which one you're in. The shift from third to fourth is also a slow one but, thanks to the fine torque characteristics of the engine and to the limitations of LOW, we chose HIGH range for all of our traffic and highway driving. The pulling power of the new DeSoto is so great that third gear is adequate for just about any hill you're likely to encounter.

Ride and Handling

Our test car weighed just under 4100 pounds and, for such a heavy machine, it rode and handled very well. The springs are soft enough to delight the typical female buyer, while Oriflo shock absorbers keep the vehicle under excellent control. Taking a severe test dip at 80 mph failed to cause the springs to bottom, but there was more recoil—more oscillating up and down—than we ever like to see.

DeSoto Road Test

Borgeson takes a tight radius turn at 50 mph, finds that while "body roll" is certainly there, it's less bothersome than in other cars of comparable weight

Sportsman hardtop, $3420 at factory

Handsome new convertible, $3850 FOB

All steel station wagon is luxurious

The car shows pronounced "roll" during fast cornering and its 7.60 x 15 tires set up quite a howl. Still, it's easy to control and its stability is fine, right up to our highest test speed of over 98 mph.

Traditional Body

The only real news in the '52 DeSoto's body is the air scoop which not only decorates the hood, but actually discharges directly against the carburetor air cleaner. The various body panels are nicely joined together and the sheet metal exposed when the doors are open is immaculate in its finish. Good workmanship is there, and it's in the paint job too: there were no runs nor was there any of the mottled texture known as orange-peel on our test car's paint.

There are many more of yesterday's ideas in the DeSoto body than there are of tomorrow's; witness the lines themselves, the twist-type door handles, and the almost-vanished cowl ventilator. The "chair-height" seats are a debatable item that get MOTOR TREND Research's approval. You sit high and have a highly useful view of the world around you. The backs of the seats are quite high, giving excellent support to the back and shoulders and this support is made perfect by just the right amount of "give" in the upholstery. Last of all, the high seats, combined with wide-opening doors, make exit and

entry a smooth operation—ladies can still look lady-like when descending from a DeSoto.

The hood and deck lids are so countersprung as to eliminate effort from the raising or lowering of either of these panels. Not so good are the facts that the outside hood latch is extremely difficult to operate and that the luggage area under the rear deck is relatively small for so large a car. The grouping of dials and controls on the instrument panel is fine but some members of our research team felt that the fully exposed, cadmium-plated sheet metal screws that hold the panel in place cheapen the appearance of that part of the car. A feature of very questionable value is the instrument panel "belly pan," a sheet metal section which extends from the bottom of the instrument panel almost to the firewall. It seems to accomplish little other than to interfere with the passengers' feet when, for example, they cross their legs.

Speaking of legs and of legroom, the tunnel in the front floorboard which encloses the DeSoto transmission is one of the largest we've ever encountered. This reduces the middle front seat passenger's legroom to a pretty uncomfortable point. Headroom, on the other hand, is plentiful for every passenger in the car.

Summary

The '52 DeSoto is a car of many contradictions: it has one of the world's best and most modern engines; its transmission keeps that engine from doing its best work; the engine that sets the pace for tomorrow propels a body that's tied to the past.

This honest evaluation of one of '52's most important cars brings out the negative, as well as the positive, facts. It tells you what to look for when you test-drive this machine. And if you're shopping for a car in this price range ($2539 to $3079, F.O.B., Detroit), be sure to give serious consideration to the DeSoto—the bugs that it doesn't have are the very features which may win you over from a competitive make.

—Griff Borgeson

DeSoto's front end shows little difference from last year's model; appearance of rear end suggests large luggage space—actually is rather small for car's size

DeSOTO ACCESSORY LIST	
FACTORY RETAIL PRICE AT FACTORY, DETROIT, MICH.	
FIRE DOME 8	
Arm rest, rear seat center (sedan only)	$ 28.75
Crankcase ventilator air cleaner	$ 1.14
Electric clock	$ 16.27
Electric window lifts (four-door sedan and station wagon)	$108.96
Electric window lifts (coupes and Sportsman)	$ 74.55
Heater, Model 504	$ 75.45
Jiffy Jet windshield washer	$ 10.34
Power brake	$ 34.49
Power steering	$185.00
Radio	$103.48
Solex glass	$ 20.00
Steering wheel, plastic	$ 11.50
Special paint	$ 40.25
Two-tone paint	$ 13.21
Transmission	
Tip-Toe shift with Fluid Drive	$122.97
Tip-Toe shift with Fluid Torque Drive	$238.97
Overdrive	$ 95.00
Wheel covers (four), stainless steel	$ 5.74

DESOTO

DeSoto has needed a new wheel-whirler for several years, and, with its so-called 160 h.p. Fire Dome 8, it's one of the hottest cars in the industry. This new rig can be bought with everything from power steering, power braking, to *shiftless* drive. In the past, DeSotos were as rugged, tough and reliable as the rock of Gibraltar, and just about as fast. With the new engine, which is a full cousin of the big V-8 Chrysler, DeSotos can now outrun 90% of the cars on the highway.

The DeSoto I tested was equipped with power steering. On the 40-mile Willow Runway, there are no speed limits and most cars cruise this between 70 and 80. On the few bends I soon found that it would be very easy to overcontrol with power steering as there was no wheel resistance at all.

DeSoto has a tiptoe shift which is a sort of semiautomatic gizmo and goes under a lot of other names in Chrysler products. It has a low and a drive range with a top gear throw-in similar to overdrive. The ride in the back seat is surprisingly un-luxurious and doesn't compare with the comfort of the front seat. The leg room in back was not mammoth and the ride was on the poor side. DeSoto has made thousands and thousands of wonderful taxis and this job rode like a hack. It is a functional ride: you won't fall out and you won't get any stone bruises, but you won't imagine you're the queen in her Rolls on her way to the Derby.

The DeSoto is a good automobile. It has proved itself among the most reliable and trouble-free cars built in America. I recommend it for anyone who wants a coast to coast cruising car or one that will stand up under a lot of abuse.

specifications:

V8, OHV, bore 3⅝"; stroke 3 11/32"; 276.1 cu. in. displacement; compression ratio 7.1 to 1; 160 h.p. at 4,400 r.p.m.; torque, 250 foot pounds at 2,000 r.p.m. Wheelbase 125½"; tread, front 56 5/16", rear 59.9/16", over-all length, 208⅜", width 74⅞", height 65⅝". Performance: 0 to 30, 5.6 seconds (in drive); 0 to 50, 10 seconds (in drive); using Low and Drive: 0 to 30, 4.2, 0 to 50, 9.1, 0 to 60, 12.2, 0 to 70, 16.6. Top speed, 96-97.

'53 DeSoto Features Entirely New Body

AN entirely new body features the 1953 DeSoto models, displayed November 13. Stylewise the longer swept-back fenders and a wider, lower rear deck result in a longer, lower and wider automobile.

The new DeSoto is offered in two series—the Fire Dome V-8, powered by the 160-h.p. Fire Dome engine—and the Powermaster Six. Both series are available with Full Power steering.

The immensity of the changeover

plant for several weeks. But the changeover time was cut to a fraction of normal by the "dress rehearsal" changeover of last summer.

Eleven body styles are offered in the two DeSoto lines. Choices in the Fire Dome V-8 include: 4-door sedan, club coupe, convertible coupe, Sportsman, all-steel station wagon and 8-passenger sedan.

Powermaster six body styles are: 4-door sedan, club coupe, Sports-

off by new large combination tail, stop and back-up lights.

A curved, one-piece windshield combined with new, narrower corner posts provides greatly increased visibility. Glass area of the windshield has been greatly increased. A one-piece, sweep-around rear window increases rear vision.

Blended into the hood line is a

Showing a functional style feature, the 1953 DeSoto's functional Air-Vent. Also the "V" below the crest on all Fire Dome V-8 models.

This is the 1953 DeSoto Fire Dome V-8 4-door sedan.

job to provide the new body was indicated recently with the revelation the division had to replace or substantially alter more than 1200 tools, machines and fixtures in its Detroit body plant.

Despite this fact, DeSoto was able to switch from 1952 to 1953

View of the 1953 DeSoto Fluid-Torque Drive.

production with a minimum of lost time in October because the task of reconverting the body plant was done during the steel strike last summer.

The new body for 1953 is altogether changed from grille to rear deck lid, from roof panel to floor plan, engineers point out. Such a complete change in body styling ordinarily closes an automobile

man, all-steel station wagon and 8-passenger sedan.

An identification highlight of the 1953 DeSoto is a massive new grille with new parking lights set at the extreme edges of the grille, underneath the headlights. A chrome frame encircles both grille and parking lights. Among styling innovations are the new chrome fender mouldings on both front and rear fenders.

Wheelbase has been maintained at 125½ inches, while overall length has been increased from 208⅜ inches to 213⅜ inches and overall width from 74⅞ inches to 76¾ inches. The car is one inch lower, but road clearance is unchanged.

Swept-back rear fenders are set

The 1953 DeSoto interior features a reflection-free panel over the top of the new dashboard between the curved, one-piece windshield and the instrument panel.

new Air-Vent, which directs a stream of cool, fresh air to the carburetor, to increase engine efficiency.

The rear deck lid is unlatched by a push-button lock and is counterbalanced for easy opening.

The trunk area of the new DeSoto has been increased by 44 percent. The spare tire, mounted at a new angle, makes it easier to store luggage. Deck lid hinges have been

Rear view of 1953 DeSoto showing wider and lower rear deck and new sweep-around rear window.

relocated in out-of-the-way positions. The gasoline tank filler cap has been located at the rear on the left side below the deck lid.

The interiors boast new uphol-

(Continued on Page 16)

SPORTSMAN Fire Dome V-8 hard-top coupe for '54 has one-piece rear window, nylon-and-leather interior. Wire wheels are optional extras.

FIRE DOME V-8 4-door Sedan has 170 h.p. with comp. ratio of 7.5. PowerFlite fully-automatic drive is offered.

PowerFlite and No-Sway Ride for De Soto

FIRE DOME V8 UPPED TO 170 H.P. IN DE SOTO AUTOMATIC FOR 1954

MORE performance and more comfort highlight the new 1954 De Soto line, which features a boost in horsepower from 160 to 170, with PowerFlite fully-automatic transmission offered as optional equipment. The new models were unveiled by dealers on November 4.

Full-Time power steering and power brakes, previous De Soto advancements, are continued as special equipment. Overdrive is available as an option with the standard 3-speed manual shift.

With a higher compression ratio of 7.5 to 1, De Soto's Fire Dome V-8 for 1954 delivers greater performance and efficiency, and its torque is improved at medium speeds, company engineers affirm. High performance stems from PowerFlite's over-all torque multiplication ratio: 4.47 to 1 in drive range, claimed the highest in the industry. The unit weighs less and has fewer parts than any other fully-automatic transmission on the market, it is pointed out by L. I. Woolson, president of De Soto. The unit consists of a new torque converter and two-speed planetary transmission. Cooling of the PowerFlite unit is by water-cooled heat exchanger on the Fire Dome V-8 and by air on the Powermaster Six.

The car can be started only with the transmission in neutral. No special position for parking is necessary on the models equipped with PowerFlite, because all De Sotos have a highly effective internal-expanding type hand brake. This brake, independent of the service brakes, operates through the drive train and will hold a car parked under any circumstance. The brake, which also may be used as an emergency brake, makes a parking sprag within the transmission unnecessary.

In exterior styling for 1954, clean body lines blend to produce a longer, wider car with a low, road-hugging look. A new "floating" grille, smoothly contoured new bumper and tail-light clusters are identification points for the new models.

Interior styling is completely new, with colors keyed to exterior finishes and new instrument panels and garnish mouldings blended with over-all color schemes.

Upholstery fabrics are offered in a variety of colors; these fabrics are, for the most part, nylon-faced for durability. Vinyl is used where soilage and scuffing are most likely to occur.

An important contribution to the new De Soto's riding comfort is No-Sway Ride Control suspension, minimizing body "lean" and eliminating tire squeal on turns, while providing improved control and all-around stability. A stiffer frame, redesigned front and rear body mountings and new rear spring mountings are also contributing factors to this new controlled ride.

Ten body styles are offered in the two De Soto lines. Choices in the Fire Dome V-8 series include: 4-Door Sedan, Club Coupe, Convertible Coupe, Sportsman, All-Steel Station Wagon and 8-Passenger Sedan. Powermaster Six body styles are: 4-Door Sedan, Club Coupe, All-Steel Station Wagon and 8-Passenger Sedan. ★

INTERIOR of 1954 De Soto Fire Dome V-8 Club Coupe includes bolstered seat design, pleated seat backs, with nylon-faced fabrics. Instrument panel is restyled.

DeSoto's Adventurer

*E*xperimental sport coupe, built on a modified, 111-inch wheelbase, DeSoto chassis by Ghia, of Turin, Italy. The engine is the 170 hp DeSoto FireDome V8 coupled to Fluid-Torque transmission. Power brakes and full-time power steering are included. Fifty-three inches to top of roof, length is 185 inches over-all.

One of the Adventurer's most interesting features, in fact, is the seating arrangement—particularly in the back. Here, two generously padded and bolstered individual 'wing' type chair seats are divided by a large, well-padded arm rest. The front seats are of similar design, but more nearly approach the conventional sport car seat. Recessed floor area provides ample leg room for rear seat passengers. ☆ ☆

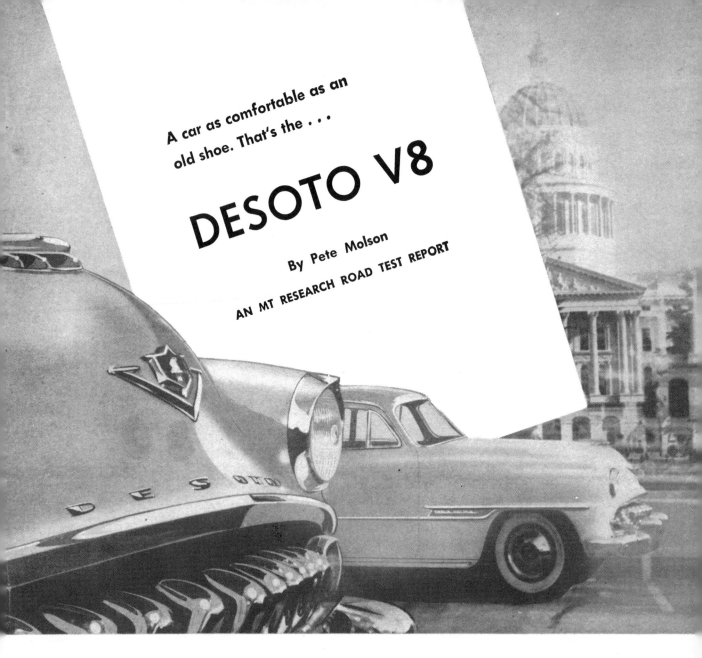

A car as comfortable as an old shoe. That's the . . .

DESOTO V8

By Pete Molson

AN MT RESEARCH ROAD TEST REPORT

WHAT DO YOU WANT in your '54 car? Lasting quality? Unstinting care in workmanship and assembly? Room to lounge, stretch out, or even wave your arms if you want to? Smooth and easy driving? Real comfort?

If these likable traits appeal to you more than flashiness, acceleration that leaves all contenders in the dust, and an interior that glitters like the latest Broad-

Like past models, the '54 Fire Dome V8 takes crises with equanimity. In the driver's seat, you'll find yourself doing the same. One of the few evidences of the work of Chrysler Chief Stylist Virgil Exner to find its way to this year's car is new dash. Round dials with their straightforward lettering show his liking for objects that don't conceal their function. Opposite page, the '53 DeSoto (small photo) and corresponding '54 model

way musical, consider a new DeSoto V8.

We don't mean that this car is any stick-in-the-mud. Far from it. Instead, without being old-fashioned, it has retained the old-fashioned virtues.

MT Research, as usual, threw the book at the test car, putting it through all sorts of unlikely trials. MT Editor Walt Woron started things off—the odometer indicated 38 miles—with a hurried 1745 mile trip through California's and Nevada's High Sierras; some of his first notes read: "Rides comfortably over the roughest roads. Accelerates well enough. Cruises well at high speeds. Finished extremely well inside and out." On his return, and as we completed our tests, the car remained unperturbed and we had no reason to list conflicting opinions.

Perhaps the first thing to strike you about the DeSoto will be its size, and it's no illusion. It's wide, long, and even a bit high by today's new standards. More important, this width, length, and height are concentrated where they are most useful: in the passenger compartment. Whether Chrysler Corp. designers are trained anatomists, we don't know, but they do a superb job of providing comfort for the people who ride in their cars.

That DeSoto's seats are not only wide but also deep and comfortably high off the floor will come as no news to fans of Chrysler-built cars; neither will the fact that there is legroom and headroom to spare and that the car is no harder to enter than the front door of your house.

Ride is generally better than in last year's car, new front suspension with non-parallel arms having brought the roll center nearer to the ideal position coincident with the center of gravity. It took some rough and tough roads to induce oscillation in the test car, but the engineers haven't licked it entirely.

We mention comfort first, because it is by all odds one of DeSoto's top features. Yet the car has acquired something of a reputation for performance since the introduction of the Fire Dome V8 engine in 1952. Does it deserve it?

By and large, yes. It's not an astounding performer, even with a 10-horsepower increase (to 170) in this year's model. But don't get the idea that we're damning it with faint praise. With the changing values of this high-performance era, our Fire Dome four-door turned in good performance figures.

Its New Transmission

To be more specific: The test car, with its more-than-satisfactory new PowerFlite transmission (DeSoto has at last bade goodbye to the outdated M-6 setup used last year) covered the standing quarter-mile in 21.4 seconds; this was 1.7 seconds slower than last year's less powerful car. The two cars had the same rear axle ratio (3.54 to 1) but the almost pointlessly low first gear of the '53 gave a terrifically powerful starting ratio when combined with the torque converter.

It may surprise you to learn that the DeSoto's ohv V8 powerplant (actually a cut-down version of the hemispherical-combustion-chamber Chrysler FirePower engine, which has lately produced well over 400 hp in experiments) is one of the smallest in its price class with its 276 cubic inches of displacement. Buick's hot Century (MT, April '54) and the newly supercharged Kaiser Manhattan now equal DeSoto's top efficiency rating (.62 hp per cubic inch) in its price class.

Chrysler V8s have amazingly low octane requirement compared to other new engines of high output. This means their engines will operate without knock on East Coast regulars. In the West they probably require a better fuel than the regulars but are more than satisfied with premium. Many other makes have difficulty on best premiums.

The safety factor for passing at highway speeds is better this year. Provided you don't abuse the privilege, it's good to know that the car will go from 50 to 80 mph in just over 19 seconds; last year's car required more than six seconds longer. Top speed is up slightly: the average of four runs was just over 99 mph.

Though lightning takeoff is not a feature of PowerFlite, there is no question that the new transmission is a vast improvement. It's smooth, uncomplicated (as automatics go) and has a shift quadrant patterned as nearly as possible after a conventional steering-post shift. In practice, this means safety when you have to think fast: for reverse, you pull toward you and flip the lever up; for low, toward you and down. The sturdy driveshaft parking brake showed no signs of weakness under the most severe tests: try as we would, we couldn't budge the De-Soto with it on. That's good, for Power-Flite-equipped cars have no provision for locking them in gear.

Its Fuel Economy

As for fuel economy, the entirely new transmission and more powerful engine produced the pleasing result of improvement across the board in all our checks. The biggest increase was to 22.5 mpg at a steady 30, an even three mpg more than last year.

The test car added still further to the Chrysler Corp. reputation for smooth and powerful brakes by noticeably improving stopping distances over its '53 counterpart (for details, see The Story in Figures, page 64). With its power brakes, De-Soto retains the conventional high pedal, contending that it is safer (by providing more leverage) if the booster should fail.

The complete story of driving and riding ease in a DeSoto is a complex one. On the test car we had the full optional

(Continued on page 16)

Photos by Tom Medley

1954 DESOTO V8 (with PowerFlite)
THE STORY IN FIGURES

PERFORMANCE

CHASSIS DYNAMOMETER TEST

(Checked on Clayton Mfg. Co.'s chassis dynamometer; all tests are made under full load, which is similar to climbing a hill at full throttle. Observed hp figures are not corrected to standard atmospheric conditions.)

RPM	MPH	ROAD HP
1350	18	34
2000	44	55
2500	58	71
2700	66	82 (maximum obtainable under any conditions)

ACCELERATION

(In seconds; checked with fifth wheel and electric speedometer)

Standing start ¼-mile (69 mph, Drive range)	21.38
0-30 mph (32, car speedometer, Drive range)	6.8
0-60 mph (65, car speedometer, Drive range)	17.93
10-30 mph (Drive range)	4.9
30-50 mph (Drive range)	6.6
50-80 mph (Drive range)	19.1

TOP SPEED

(In miles per hour; clocked over surveyed ¼-mile)

Fastest one-way run	101.4
Slowest one-way run	96.8
Average of four runs	99.0

FUEL CONSUMPTION

(In miles per gallon; checked with fuel flow-meter, fifth wheel, and electric speedometer)

Steady 30 mph	20.2
Steady 45 mph	19.2
Steady 60 mph	15.9
Steady 75 mph	13.3
Simulated traffic over measured course	12.9
Total mileage driven and overall average for entire test	2623 @ 15.2

BRAKE STOPPING DISTANCE

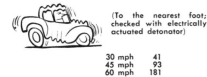

(To the nearest foot; checked with electrically actuated detonator)

30 mph	41
45 mph	93
60 mph	181

PRICES

(Including retail price at main factory, federal tax, and delivery and handling charges, but not freight)

	Six	V8
Four-door sedan	$2386	$2673
Club coupe	2364	2652
Hardtop		2923
Convertible		3144
Station wagon	3108	3381
Eight-passenger sedan	3281	3559

ACCESSORIES

Automatic transmission	$189
Overdrive	98
Power steering	140
Power brakes	37
Radio	101
Heater	78
Direction signals	Standard
Backup lights	Standard
Air conditioning	643
White sidewall tires (additional cost per set)	33

GENERAL SPECIFICATIONS

ENGINE

Type	V8, laterally inclined ohv
Bore & stroke	3⅝ x 3 11/32
Stroke/bore ratio	0.92 to 1
Compression ratio	7.5 to 1
Displacement	276.1 cu. in.
Advertised bhp	170 @ 4400 rpm
Bhp per cu. in.	.62
Piston travel @ max. bhp	2452 ft. per min.
Maximum torque	255 lbs.-ft. @ 2400 rpm
Maximum bmep	139 psi

DRIVE SYSTEM

Standard transmission	Three-speed synchromesh using helical gears
Ratios	1st 2.57, 2nd 1.83, 3rd 1.00, reverse 3.48
Automatic transmission	PowerFlite, torque converter with gears
Ratios	Low 1.72 x converter ratio, drive 1.72 and 1.00 x converter ratio, reverse 2.39 x converter ratio; maximum converter ratio at stall, 2.6 @ 1325 rpm
Overdrive transmission	Planetary type with manual lockout and accelerator downshift
Ratio	0.7 to 1 (overall 2.87)
Rear axle ratios	Conventional 3.73, automatic 3.54, overdrive 4.1

DIMENSIONS

Wheelbase	125½ in.
Tread	Front 56 5/16, rear 59⅝ in.
Wheelbase/tread ratio	2.17
Overall width	77⅝ in.
Overall length	214½ in.
Overall height	62½ in.
Turning diameter	41 ft. 9 in.
Turns lock to lock	3 (power steering) 5 (conventional)
Test car weight	4040 lbs. (factory shipping wt. 3950 lbs.)
Test car weight/bhp ratio	23.8 to 1
Weight distribution	Front 57%, rear 43%
Tire size	7.60 x 15
Tire loading	Front 100%, rear 77%

DEPRECIATION

These figures will be given in a future issue. In the interest of accuracy, MT Research is re-evaluating the method of figuring depreciation.

ESTIMATED COST PER MILE

These figures will be given in a future issue. In the interest of accuracy, MT Research is re-evaluating the method of figuring estimated cost per mile.

PARTS AND LABOR COST

These figures will be given in a future issue. various repairs and replacements. Your car may require all of them in a short time, or it may require none. However, a comparison of prices for these sample operations in various makes is often of interest to prospective owners.

	PARTS	LABOR
Distributor	$ 41.13	$ 4.00
Battery	19.95	
Fuel pump	10.00	2.80
Valve grind	6.28	45.20
One front fender	44.95	18.00
Bumper	78.05	4.50
Two tires	57.50	
TOTALS	$257.86	$74.50

(Continued from page 15)

equipment: automatic shift, power steering, power brakes. As for the power steering, we list these points in its favor: unequaled ease of operation; no change in driver effort under different conditions; quick ratio. Against it are its complete lack of road feel and its difficulty of operation if the engine stalls.

Its Past Reputation

Over the years, DeSoto has built up a well-deserved reputation for being as comfortable as an old shoe (without looking like one). This year an icily handsome new instrument panel is one of the most noticeable changes. It's excellent in concept but needs more attention from the designers for daytime driving, when reflections and lack of contrast make it tough to read.

The driver comfort list is lengthened by such items as a mirror that adjusts for height; a nonglare, vinyl-topped dash; the easiest manual window lifts in the industry (also the safest, because of their speed, if you ever need a window opened or closed in a hurry); back-up lights; constant-speed electric wipers; direction signals, and a trunk light; MT is especially pleased to report that everything in that list—plus an oil-bath air cleaner—is a standard item at no extra cost on every 1954 DeSoto.

DeSoto still offers its Powermaster models, powered by the conventional L-head, long-stroke Six. Interiors are simpler, and there the differences end. Some $300 less, these cars are good buys for those who don't need high performance.

It's not exaggerating to say that MT thinks you'll still be pleased if you keep your DeSoto for 10 years. It's no summer soldier.

—*Pete Molson*

De Soto for 1953

(Continued from Page 11)

stery fabrics, harmonized with new interior trim and body color.

A distinctive interior touch on the new models is a reflection-free panel over the top of the dashboard between the windshield and the instrument panel.

The 1953 DeSoto has a new heating system. Mounted under a new cowl vent opening, the heater takes in fume-free fresh air. The cowl vent is also used for summer cooling. The heater features a new design with simplified controls which permit operation as a recirculating heater as well as one which supplies a constant stream of fresh, warm air.

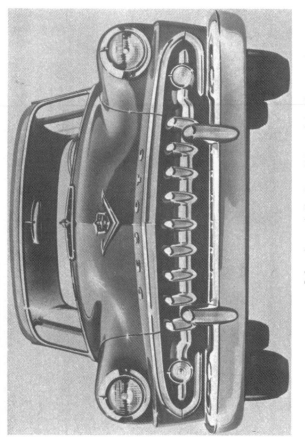

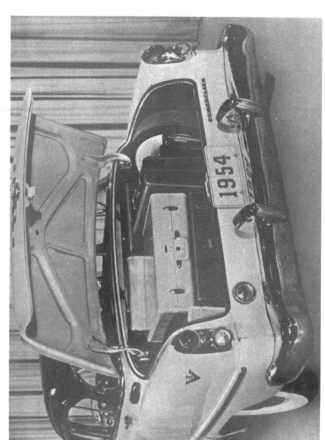

DeSOTO

DeSoto Automatic Fire Dome V-8, restyled with massive bumper and guards, new hooded headlights and parking lights set in either end of grille. Other features are large trunk, contoured rear bumper, taillight clusters including stop light, back-up light, turn signals in single unit

"The most powerful engine design in the world," is the claim given the Fire Dome engine by its engineers. The V-8 170-horsepower engine, with a compression ratio of 7.5 to 1, is featured in six models of the 1954 De Soto. These include the four-door sedan, club coupe, Sportsman, convertible coupe, all-steel station wagon and eight-passenger sedan.

In the Powermaster "six" series there are four body styles: four-door sedan, club coupe, all-steel station wagon and eight-passenger sedan. Each of these is driven by the Powermaster six-cylinder L-head engine, developing 116 horsepower at 3600 r.p.m.

POWERFLITE TRANSMISSION

The automatic transmission, featured on the 1954 De Soto, weighs less and has fewer parts than any other fully automatic transmission, according to L. I. Woolson, president of De Soto. PowerFlite has been engineered with a new torque converter and two-speed planetary transmission. Cushioning effect of the oil in the torque converter and one automatic shift from starting gear to direct drive give an exceptionally smooth operation to the new PowerFlite transmission.

The single fully automatic shift from starting gear to direct drive takes place between 15 and 65 m.p.h., depending upon acceleration by the driver. If more speed is wanted after the transmission is in direct drive, the driver may "kick down" to low gear by pressing the accelerator to the floorboard. PowerFlite also automatically "downshifts" any time the car speed falls below 11 m.p.h. This new transmission is optional equipment on all models in both Fire Dome V-8 and Powermaster Six series of De Soto.

STYLING

Throughout both lines of 1954 De Sotos, interiors and exteriors have been completely restyled with upholstery fabrics and colors. Woven patterns and solid-color materials are used. Leatherlike vinyls, blended into the over-all scheme, are placed where soiling and scuffing might occur.

The Sportsman and convertible models feature leathers in pastel shades contrasted with darker seat cloths carrying a lightly dotted pattern. These can be styled in five different color plans to please the most discriminating tastes. Seat styling and construction have been entirely changed to give the greatest possible comfort for the motorist.

HIGHLIGHTS

An important development on the new De Soto is the No-Sway Ride Control suspension, minimizing body lean and eliminating tire squeal on turns, while providing improved control and all-around stability. A stiffer frame, redesigned front and rear body mountings and rear-spring mountings are also contributing factors in this new controlled ride.

Every De Soto includes as standard equipment: two-speed electric windshield wipers, dual back-up lights, directional signals, a luggage-compartment light, oil-bath air cleaner and Oilite fuel filter. All models are equipped with Safety-Rim wheels for maximum protection in case of tire failure. De Soto full-time power steering, available as optional equipment, is in operation while the engine is running and reduces steering effort by 80 percent.

Colors available on the De Soto automatic are: black, ensign blue, azure blue, Huron blue, colonial gray, slate gray, Kerry green, forest green, Pinehurst green, Burma tan and Arizona beige.

A newly styled and improved air-vent hood on the De Soto directs a stream of cool, fresh air to the carburetor for increased engine efficiency. De Soto is claimed to have been the first American car to feature a functional hood vent.

De Soto's Airtemp air conditioning system has a cooling capacity equivalent to melting 6000 lbs. of ice in 24 hrs.

17

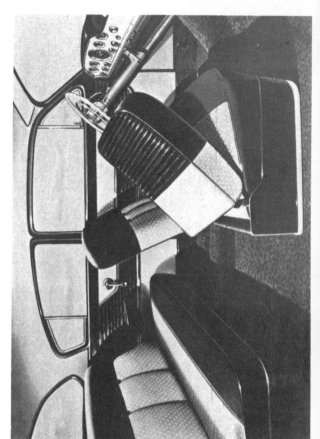

Fire Dome V-8 club coupe emphasizes the longer, wider appearance of the DeSoto Automatic. Powerflite automatic transmission is optional. Instrument panel and garnish moldings (below) harmonize with over-all color scheme. A wide range of interior colors and trim is available

DeSOTO

1954 DESOTO SPECIFICATIONS

GENERAL

	POWERMASTER "6"	FIREDOME "8"
Wheelbase	125 1/2	125 1/2
Over-all height	62 1/2	62 1/2
Over-all width	77 5/8	77 5/8
Over-all length	214 1/2	214 1/2
Tread, front	56 5/16	56 5/16
Tread, rear	59 5/8	59 5/8
Turning diameter	41' 7"	41' 7"

ENGINE

	POWERMASTER "6"	FIREDOME "8"
Type	6-Cylinder	8-Cylinder
	In-line	V-head
	L-head	OHV
Bore and stroke	3 7/16 x 4 1/2	3 5/8 x 3 11/32
Piston displacement	250.6 cu. in.	276.1 cu. in.
Compression ratio	7.0 to 1	7.5 to 1
Maximum horsepower	116 at 3600 r.p.m.	170 at 4400 r.p.m.
Taxable horsepower	28.36	42.05
Transmission (Conventional)	Standard	Standard
(Overdrive)	Optional	Optional
(Automatic)	Optional	Optional

BODY DIMENSIONS

	POWERMASTER "6"	FIREDOME "8"
Front-seat width	61 1/2	61 1/2
Rear-seat width	60 1/8	60 1/8
Shoulder room, front	57	57
Shoulder room, rear	54 1/2	54 1/2
Leg room, font	44	44
Leg room, rear	41 7/8	41 7/8
Headroom, front	36 1/4	36 1/4
Headroom, rear	35 1/4	35 1/4

TIRE DIMENSIONS

	POWERMASTER "6"	FIREDOME "8"
Standard	7.60 x 15.4	7.60 x 15.4
Optional	7.60 x 15.6	7.60 x 15.6
(front)	24 lbs.	24 lbs.
Inflation (rear)	24 lbs.	24 lbs.

CAPACITIES

	POWERMASTER "6"	FIREDOME "8"
Water (less heater)	15 qts.	22 qts.
Oil (less filter)	5 qts.	5 qts.
Gasoline	17 gal.	17 gal.

Rear seat of the station wagon folds into the floor to provide more cargo space. Upholstery is plaid pattern with vinyl bolsters

DeSOTO

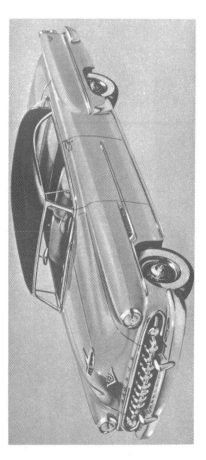

DeSoto Fire Dome V-8 club coupe features one-piece rear window and an interior of pleated nylon color-harmonized with leather bolsters. The same body style is also offered in the Powermaster "Six" series (below). Powerflite transmission is available on either series of new models

Fire Dome V-8 Sportsman features wire wheels, Powerflite, power steering, power brakes, electric window lifts and air conditioning as optional

Four-door sedan is equipped with Fire Dome engine stepped up to 170 horsepower. Safety-Rim wheels are standard equipment on all models. Silhouette lighting makes only the instruments' numerals and pointers appear lighted. Each instrument has its own separate circular dial

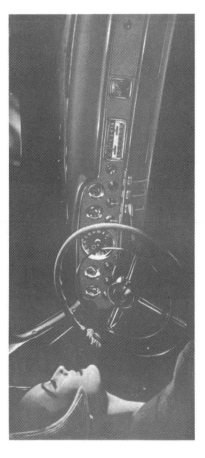

Another of the Chrysler family's pride and joys, DeSoto's Adventurer II is the second superb Ghia car to bear the name

Rear window is actually sliding roof section. Visible are bucket seats, built-in luggage strapped onto the rear shelf

Sharply accented rear end takes on jet-like appearance with chrome-rimmed tail lights. Metal body was crafted in Italy

New Ghia DeSoto

THE ADVENTURER II, with its pronounced "tumblehome" (inward sloping superstructure) and almost horizontal rear window, bears little resemblance to its predecessor (MT, Jan. '54).

Our guess is that Virgil Exner (Chrysler Corp.'s Styling Director) had very little to do with the design of this car. The slab sides and the illusion of excessive width violate the Exner trademark, which is emphasis on the mechanical beauty and function of an automobile.

We saw this one recently, and Ghia's craftsmanship is superb. So far, the trend on this side of the ocean towards Fiberglas show cars (GM, Packard, and Ford) serves mostly to highlight the superior skill of the Italian master body-builder who seldom works with more than just a sheet of raw metal and a hammer.

Compulsory Safety Check

WITH THE SIGNATURE of Gov. Thomas E. Dewey on a law effective July 1, 1954 New York became the 14th state to make motor vehicle inspection compulsory.

One of the toughest auto legislations in the country, the new law will provide semi-annual inspection of over four million vehicles. Covered in the inspection will be brakes, steering, wheel alignment, horns, tires, lights, glass, windshield wipers, and other equipment. Inspection will be carried out at state-licensed garages, a procedure common to all but two states, and the District of Columbia, where state-owned-and-operated stations are utilized.

A nationwide survey shows 15 other states which permit their cities to conduct vehicle inspection. Among the cities with active ordinances are Evanston, Ill., Des Moines, Iowa, and Miami, Fla.

Gov. Dewey, in signing New York's inspection bill, said, "Periodic inspection focuses attention on the condition of the motor vehicle. It helps rid the roads of death traps on wheels which menace the lives and property of other motorists and pedestrians . . ."

FULL DETAILS: '55 DESOTO...

DeSoto retains familiar appearance, has no unsightly styling gimmicks for '55

Fireflite Sportsman hardtop has sidespear painted to match the color of top

Good-looking instrument panel is DeSoto feature. Brake pedal is eight inches wide, virtually calls for left-foot application

Torsion bar system balances trunk lid at any angle. Hinges are well out of the way, will greatly reduce luggage damage

THERE WAS A TIME when DeSoto could be called the experimental car of the Chrysler Corp. Do you remember the 1942 model with its fold-away headlights? After the war, this division became the most conservative member of a family that tended to be pretty pro-status quo anyway.

NOW DESOTO IS OUT FOR BEAR with their striking new 200-horsepower Fireflite series. Like all the new Exner-designed cars, it is clean, slim, and looks like a real automobile. Ornamentation is used not to create new highlights but to accentuate existing ones. When you get in, you face the best-looking instrument panel we have seen on any new car to date. Fabrics are "dope-dyed" for color stability.

FIREFLITE AND FIRE DOME MODELS (185 horsepower) share the same 126-inch wheelbase chassis which has full length, box section side rails, a stronger front crossmember, and rear springs made parallel (and over five inches farther apart) by outrigging the front shackle. Convertible-coupe cowl shake, chronic on all earlier Chrysler-built cars, has been tackled this year by using a special frame incorporating I-beams for the X-members, rather than the previously used U channels. Roll center (the point about which the car naturally tends to tilt) is one of the highest in the industry.

COWL-SUSPENDED BRAKE (AND CLUTCH) PEDALS, long overdue on all Chrysler products, are offered for the first time. The power brake option has a six-inch pedal travel with new valving that eases surge when the power cuts in. PowerFlite-equipped DeSotos have what is easily the industry's broadest brake pedal, and the excellent internal-expanding handbrake is continued on all models. Chrysler Corp. considers this good enough to eliminate the need for a parking pawl in PowerFlite, greatly simplifying that transmission.

Photos by Dean Moon

Three pictures show some of handling and braking maneuvers DeSoto underwent during testing of 1955 FireFlite four-door.

ROAD TEST

DE SOTO
FIREFLITE

It's new and different, with performance to match the luxury and ease of driving

DE SOTO has the new "forward look" inside and out for 1955, along with extensive engineering changes in the chassis and engine compartment. These all add up to a distinctively different car from the one that bore the same name in the previous year.

Newest name in the DeSoto lineup is the FireFlite, the top series that features more luxury, refinements and power than anything else DeSoto has offered in a big production model during its 27-year history. So it was the natural choice for a road test in the popular four-door sedan body type.

The FireFlite's fresh styling can be noted in the photos, while the basic specifications are contained in the box on the opposite page. Performance figures, too,

can be checked at a glance. But none of these tell the whole story, so let's get behind the wheel and go.

A heftier 200-hp version of the V-8 engine obviously effects a reduction in acceleration times over previous years. Most of the punch, however, appears in the middle speed ranges. Runs under the clock starting alternately in drive and low produced no significant results. When floorboarding the gas pedal with the selector lever in low, it was noted that the FireFlite peaks out at an actual 70 mph.

Since the DeSoto was loaded with power accessories, such as steering, brakes and so forth, the testers conducted a modest experiment. Disconnecting the power steering, for instance, showed an improvement of one to two seconds in

the time for the quarter-mile from a standing start. It points up the penalty an owner has to pay for the comforts of such conveniences on any car.

The increased performance has been obtained from the V-8 without changing the compression ratio from last year's 7.5-to-1, which causes economical regular gasoline to remain the recommended fuel. Instead, DeSoto engineers chose to boost the displacement by nearly 15 cubic inches, employ larger intake and higher-lift exhaust valves, and go from a dual to a four-barrel carburetor. Maximum torque is now 274 ft. lbs. at 2800 rpm, in contrast to the previous 255 at 2400. Advertised horsepower is 200, a gain of 30 horsepower over 1954.

At top speed, which averages out to

22

105 mph, the DeSoto moves easily and handles well. A four-inch wider tread and lower center of gravity, plus the streamlining of the new body style, make the chief contributions to control and security. The full-time power steering helps iron out the road bumps and very little shock is transmitted to the driver's wheel.

Handling during sharp cornering and on winding roads also is a big improvement over the 1954 models. The design changes which influence this include a lower spring rate, new steering gear, widening the rear spring mounts and improving the Oriflow shocks. This makes the DeSoto ride soft, while tightening up on the roll and sway.

During the panic-stop tests for braking effectiveness, the DeSoto screeched to a halt in a distance that was average for its weight and class. And nosedive obviously had been reduced. Pedal pressure actuating the power brake system was soft, without sudden grabs, while the pad surface was wide, designed for either right or left foot use, and on a plane close to the throttle pedal for easy pivoting.

From behind the wheel, the DeSoto's seating, among the best in the business, is ideal for long-distance over-the-road cruising. Aided by the power seat, the driver has good vision over the lower

SPECIFICATIONS	
Engine type	OHV / V-8
Displacement	291 cubic inches
BHP	200 @ 4400 rpm
Compression ratio	7.5-TO-1
Bore 3.27	Stroke 3.34
Torque 274 ft.-lbs. @ 2800 rpm	
Transmission	PowerFlite
Rear axle ratio	3.54
Wheelbase	126 inches
Dry weight	4300 lbs.
Turning circle	46 feet
Steering lock-to-lock	3.5 turns

PRICES	
Car $2498	Power Steering $113
Transmission Automatic $178	Power Brakes $40
Radio $110-$128	Air Conditioning
Heater $92	$567

wheel and through the distortion-free curved glass. Nice touch: positioning the electric window lift controls well forward to reduce cramping the arm to reach them. Like other Chrysler Corporation cars, the selector quadrant and gear lever are on the dash—a step in the right direction which other manufacturers will follow, with further refinement eliminating present minor blind spots.

Since the DeSoto features an entirely new body, a close look reveals improvements made other than styling. Major changes in dimensions are three inches increase in overall length, a two-inch reduction in height, and a 4.5-inch increase in interior hip room. Whelbase and overall width are about the same as 1954. Despite reduction in overall height, there's practically no loss in interior headroom.

Exit and entry, front or back, is easy with doors that open wide. Door handles are a novel touch (see photo). Other interior appointments are colorful and lush. Neat trick is concealment of the forward cigaret lighter within the ash tray. Location of the clock could be improved by recessing it into the dash; otherwise, the dash arrangement is excellent, with a style unlike any other car and one that should be retained. Glove compartment is near center, is deeper and has recessed bottom to prevent contents from spilling when door is opened.

With a full load of accessories and equipment, the FireFlite's cost per pound, according to DeSoto, makes it less than such staple items of food as steak and coffee. The comparison is a good one, since DeSoto is a lot of car for the money and any driver will find plenty of pleasure in every ounce. ●

MOTOR LIFE ROAD TEST

CAR TESTED: 1955 DeSoto FireFlite 4-Dr. Sedan	

TEST CONDITIONS	
Altitude	200 feet
Temperature	66 degrees
Wind	14 mph
Gasoline	Mobilgas Premium

ACCELERATION AND TOP SPEED

MPH	0-30	0-45	0-60	30-50	40-60
Seconds	4.5	8.4	12.5	5	6.2

Standing ¼ mile	19 seconds
Fastest one-way run	107.2 mph
Top speed avg. 4 runs	105 mph

SPEEDOMETER CORRECTIONS		BRAKING DISTANCE	
Car Speedometer	Actual Speeds	MPH	Stopping Distance
20	17	30	41 feet
30	28	45	87 feet
40	36	60	139 feet
50	45		
60	54	FUEL CONSUMPTION	
70	65	MPH	Average
80	72	30	20 mpg
90	83	45	18.5 mpg
100	—	60	17.5 mpg

REMARKS: BRAKING AND ACCELERATION TESTS MADE ON DRY PAVEMENT.

Door handles are recessed. Pressure on button causes lever to project for opening. One of many novel touches on car.

DeSoto gets good mileage on regular gasoline, with compression ratio the same as last year. Body is longer, lower.

Jacking car for tire changes is important. On DeSoto it's easy with notched locations for secure grip to avoid slip.

Dash is genuinely unique in styling, has sporty look. Glove compartment is deep and located just to right of radio dials.

MT RESEARCH road test

DeSoto pulls down under maximum deceleration, keeps bumper well above the road surface. Stopped straight, fade-free

by Jim Lodge

YOU WON'T ALWAYS find exciting phraseology and impressive performance in MT's road test reports, but you will find something that does come up with striking consistency in the write-ups on the DeSotos—improvement of details from year to year in nearly every respect. It's a car that has yet to swap a time-honored reputation earned as a subdued-but-willing family car for the glamour of new car sales appeal.

Test car: A 4-door sedan, 200-hp Fireflite series. PowerFlite transmission, power steering, and power brakes, automatic seat adjustment, and power window lifts.

Engine: Upped 30 hp from last year, ohv V8 retains original Chrysler hemispherical combustion chambers but now mounts 4-barrel carburetor. Displacement greater by 14.9 inches (now 291 cubic inches), torque now 274 foot-pounds. Intake and exhaust valves are larger than in '54, valves lift higher.

Other options: You name it, the DeSoto dealer has the optional equipment. Alternate basic car is less powerful (185 hp), less deluxe, less expensive, but wholly satisfactory FireDome DeSoto. It uses the lower-ratio gearing of '54 DeSoto 6 with all transmissions: its PowerFlite axle is 3.73, should give no better economy, fair performance at low speeds, not equal to Fireflite at any speed. Synchromesh, with or without overdrive, available in either.

What the car is like to drive: It's comparable to the '55 Dodge (see road test in March MT), which means real easy. Good-sized wheel, comfortable driver position, plenty of vision fore and aft. New double cowl design is real sporty, has a great future. Clock should be first to go with modifications; purists will term it unsafe, most call it awkward. DeSoto has had better setups for quick-glance instrument legibility than golden numerals that blend with background.

PowerFlite panel control lever has been worked over in early reports from Detroit on all Chrysler Corp. products, and in our Plymouth and Dodge road tests. But here's something new: We didn't like the way DeSoto's lever aimed its tapered plastic tip at passengers, and questioned Chrysler Engineering about it. We found

Easy-to-release safety catch is under air-scoop slot; hood is light but well braced

the lever is made of SAE 1010 steel, soft grade that bends easily. About 10 pounds force will snap lever off flush with or slightly below surface of panel. As double precaution, lever is dog-legged, or bent, so it'll bend or break just right!

With that cleared up, on to driving. Brake pedal is fairly high (for leverage), but more vital, it's usable for left or right foot braking. Nothing new about accelerator except car's response to it.

Ease of handling: Smooth, quiet, no work involved. Don't worry about getting used to the DeSoto. No-muscle steering eases car out of streetcar tracks, out of ruts or soft shoulders with hardly a movement in the wheel. Car is big and heavy; try wheeling into a tight, hard turn—then recover with or without throt-

tle action. No matter how, it's easy. Maybe you misjudged car or parking place. If you got halfway in and have to work out again, you won't need a shower.

Acceleration: Take-off was smooth and easy, but it carried some authority. Comparative analysis: '54 car 0-60 in 17.9, standing quarter-mile in 21.3; '55 test car 0-60 in 12.8, the quarter in 19.2 seconds. Using LOW in the 0-60 runs won't get you there any quicker; DRIVE does

the same all by itself, shifting out of LOW just at 60. In a longer run, LOW does the most if held in up to about 65-68 mph.

We don't know anyone who buys his family car for top speed; but if you're interested in the DeSoto from age-old-argument standpoint, it averages 103. Down where power counts, acceleration is good. This year's DeSoto cut about 5 seconds off its former 50-80 time. Low speed acceleration is boosted by Power-Flite design change. Smaller diameter torque converter allows higher engine speeds for more getaway power.

Braking: Straight-line pull-down, little fade. Brake checks a no-fuss, no-muss proposition inciting one comment: Has least amount of nose-dive among Chrysler-built cars (said prior to the Chrysler New Yorker road test). Credit newly positioned shock absorbers, decent weight distribution. Stopping power for '55 better across the board, big improvement at 60 mph.

Roadability: Consider riding quality here: with this in mind, roadability rates genuinely good. Sticks in curves with confidence (on behalf of both driver and car); heel-over is there, not sloppy. Front end inclined to wash out when things get fast and rough; never reached the critical point in our 50-65 mph constant-curve tests. At these speeds comes a tire-moaning drift with rear end right in line with front. Don't look for needle-sharp precision in car controls. Do look for DeSoto's help in keeping you out of trouble.

Behind tales of roadability lie these facts: As in Plymouth and Dodge setups, Oriflow shocks have much freedom, now contribute more to suspension in ride and directional stability. Along with Chrysler

and Imperial, DeSoto has nearly 4 inches wider front tread. Redesigned, well-braced frame puts rear springs more than 5 inches farther apart than in '54.

No wander coming out of dips, little or no rebound. Snakes across washboard roads like it had eyes. Some body movement, but at worst, it's transmitted thru wheels to vibration in driver's hands. Take your hands off the wheel (with a last twist for good measure) and the DeSoto explores its way back to straight and narrow without heading for the nearest ditch.

Ride: Definitely in style, definitely top feature in '55 Fireflite. Excellent compromise in a car noted for upholding pillowy ride of the Chrysler line. Sidesway not too noticeable—even to Lonesome George riding in the rear seat by himself. He'll sit fairly steady, won't slide too much on turns, won't pitch to the ceiling in a highway hole, won't get that rising-elevator sensation in a shallow dip. Long-liked DeSoto seats add firmness as well as long-trip comfort. Floor-to-seat, seat-to-seatback setup means 50-75 miles more before a rest stop.

What the car is like to live with: Like good-quality materials, a touch of glitter, plenty of living-room comfort? It's here. Things that'll impress you: Plenty of room to move around; wide-opening doors for easy entry and exit; nylon loop pile floor mats (sponge-rubber backed), quiet, soft; nylon and vinyl upholstery and trim, colorful, durable, up-to-date; bright map-reading or courtesy lights up under each panel cowl; larger glove compartment this year. Livability isn't limited to passenger compartment; trunk space is family-size, finish, loading ease average.

rille remains customizers' gold mine (they like the "teeth"), ides hood latch. Chrome is lavish per sales demands

And here's the crux of the sequence: A flat hood without head-denting overhang makes it easy to work on Fireflite V8

Panel-mounted shift lever is contacted about where column shift would be touched. See text for unusual shift lever detail

Doors open to nearly 90 degrees for easy entry, exit. Car is almost 2 inches lower than '54, headroom is only ¾-inch less

'55 DESOTO FIREFLITE

Economy and ease of maintenance: Do-it-yourself fans can cut costs; engine components and accessories fairly accessible, there for all to see or dismantle. Valve train ready for service; carburetion, ignition, other components little different from other ohv V8s in accessibility. Sparkplugs hard to remove.

If MT's test car indicates what you'll be getting, you'll be happy with general detailing inside and out. Good paint job, normal tattoo of file marks barely discernible on door posts, quarter panels. Good fit to upholstery, trim; not-so-good fit where windshield molding meets instrument panel. But no squeaks or rattles. Here's a tip: The DeSoto held up unusually and remarkably well under some of the roughest tryouts we've given *any* car on our test courses.

Fuel economy: Don't look for economy in your weekly tank mileage; instead, you'll probably find it in the year-end tally of maintenance costs. Steady-speed fuel economy off slightly this year. Tank average lower, primarily because the 2 vacuum-actuated barrels on the carburetor give more pep (you're inclined to lead-foot a livelier car), take extra gas in the process. (Except for mentioned change in PowerFlite, drive train is like '54s, with 3.54 rear axle ratio.) But by using regular grade gas (we used Mobilgas Regular in all the tests) as recommended by the manufacturer, you can apply the pennies to vacation costs or sundry costs peculiar to Mr. Average Motorist.

GENERAL SPECIFICATIONS

ENGINE: Ohv V8. Bore 3.27 in. Stroke 3.344 in. Stroke/bore ratio 0.899:1. Compression ratio 7.5 to 1. Displacement 291 cu. in. Advertised bhp 200 @ 4400 rpm. Bhp per cu. in. 0.687. Piston travel @ max. bhp 2452 ft. per min. Max. bmep 138.2 psi. Max. torque 274 ft.-lb. @ 2800 rpm.

DRIVE SYSTEM: STANDARD transmission is 3-speed synchromesh using helical gears. RATIOS: 1st 2.57, 2nd 1.83, 3rd 1.00, reverse 3.48. AUTOMATIC transmission is PowerFlite, 3-element torque converter with planetary gears. RATIOS: Drive 1.72 x converter ratio and converter only; Low, 1.72 x converter ratio; Reverse 2.39 x converter ratio. Maximum converter ratio at stall 2.6. OVERDRIVE transmission is standard shift with planetary gears. RATIO: 0.7.

REAR AXLE RATIOS: Standard 3.73, PowerFlite 3.54, Overdrive 4.1.

DIMENSIONS: Wheelbase 126 in. Tread 60.2 front, 59.6 rear. Wheelbase/tread ratio 2.10:1. Overall width 78.3 in. Overall length 217.9 in. Overall height (empty) 62.7 in. Turning diameter 46 ft. 4 in. Turns lock to lock 5.5 (3.5 with power steering). Test car weight 4300 lbs. Test car weight/bhp ratio 21.5:1. Weight distribution 54.2% front, 45.8% rear. Tire size 7.60 x 15 tubeless.

PRICES: (Including suggested retail price at main factory, federal tax, and delivery and handling charges, but not freight) FIREDOME 4-door sedan $2498, hardtop $2541 and $2654, convertible $2824. FIREFLITE 4-door sedan $2727, hardtop $2939, convertible $3151.

ACCESSORIES: PowerFlite $178, overdrive $108, power package $40, radios $110 and $128, heater $92, power steering $113, power brakes $40, power seat $70, power windows $102, air conditioning $567.

TEST CAR AT A GLANCE

'55 DeSoto Fireflite with PowerFlite

REAR WHEEL HORSEPOWER
(Determined on Clayton chassis dynamometer. All tests are made under full load, which is similar to climbing a hill at full throttle. Observed hp figures not corrected to standard atmospheric conditions.)

59 road hp @ 1700 rpm and 23 mph
72 road hp @ 2000 rpm and 38 mph
88 road hp @ 2500 rpm and 58 mph
Max. 105 road hp @ 3025 rpm and 72 mph

TOP SPEED
(In miles per hour over surveyed ¼-mile.)

Fastest 1-way run	106.0
Slowest 1-way run	101.1
Average of 4 runs	103.2

ACCELERATION
(In seconds, checked with 5th wheel and electric speedometer.)

Standing start ¼-mile (76 mph)	19.2
0-30 mph	4.3
0-60 mph	12.8
10-30 mph	3.6
30-50 mph	4.9
50-80 mph	14.3

SPEEDOMETER ERROR
(Checked with 5th wheel and electric speedometer.)

Car speedometer read 32 @ true 30 mph
48 @ true 45 mph
63 @ true 60 mph
79 @ true 75 mph
108 @ top speed

FUEL CONSUMPTION
(In miles per gallon; checked with fuel flow-meter, 5th wheel, and electric speedometer. Mobilgas Regular used.)

Steady 30 mph	19.7
Steady 45 mph	18.2
Steady 60 mph	15.7
Steady 75 mph	11.9
Stop-and-go driving over measured course	12.4
Tank average for 613 miles	12.2

STOPPING DISTANCE
(To the nearest foot; checked with electrically actuated detonator.)

30 mph	39
45 mph	90
60 mph	146

New features on this 250-horsepower Fireflite 4-door sedan are tubeless tires, New Horizon full wrap-around windshield, "Flite Control" gear selector mounted on the dash, and a low-silhouette body design.

DESOTO

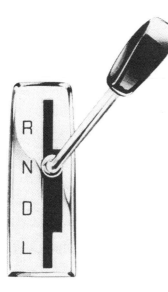

The control lever for automatic shift is now located on the dash.

'Styled for Tomorrow' describes the Fireflite and the Firedome models, which boast a host of design and engineering changes.

ALL new from every view" is the way De Soto describes its line of automobiles for 1955. They are the Fireflite series of four-door sedans, Sportsman hardtops and convertible coupes powered by the new Fireflite 200 horsepower hemispheric combustion chamber V-8 engine, and the equally new Firedome series with a V-8 engine rated at 185 horsepower.

Firedome models include a four-door sedan, Sportsman hardtop, convertible coupe, Special coupe, and station wagon.

The eight new De Soto models for 1955, the company claims, are dimentionally and statistically the longest, lowest, roomiest and most powerful in the history of the firm (exclusive of special purpose vehicles).

Built on a newly designed chassis with a wheelbase of 126 inches, the new models have an overall length of 217.9 inches; height has been reduced in the four-door models to 60.6 inches and to 59.9 inches in the hardtops and convertibles; hip room and leg room has been substantially increased in all models, with front seats over 64 inches wide and driver leg room measuring more than 44 inches.

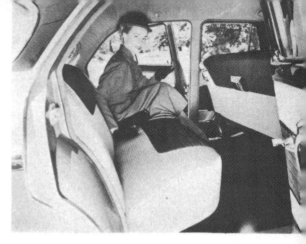

'Beauty-curved' rear window adds to the lines of the 1955 model.

There is a choice of thirty-nine inside trim-fabric combinations.

In the Fireflite Series, a four-door sedan and a Sportsman hardtop coupe are offered, along with the convertible coupe, shown above. Power plant is a 200-horsepower hemispherical combustion V-8 engine.

The Fireflite Sportsman hardtop coupe is a new De Soto entry this year. Automatic transmission, power brakes, Airtemp air conditioning, coaxial-type power steering and electric window-lifts are introduced.

"All new from every view" is the way DeSoto describes its Firedome models. Shown at right is the brilliantly styled four-door sedan. At lower right is the station wagon.

New Features Offered

Among the new exterior features that distinguish the 1955 models are new body lines expressive of power and performance, a massive grille integrated with the bumper, recessed headlights with a distinct Continental flair, functional air scoop incorporating the De Soto emblem, full wrap-around "New Horizon" windshield that gives driver complete range of vision at eye level where it is needed, "Sun Cap" visor of heavy chrome, a javelin-like chrome strip running the full length of the car, accentuating body highlights, and semi-flush push-pull door handles.

Thirteen solid colors and 42 two-tone combinations are available. Interiors offer 39 trim combinations in a choice of patterns—nylons, vinyls, buffed and grained leathers. Fireflite carpets are luxurious and colorful of heavy denier nylon loop pile backed by a thick layer of sponge rubber.

The instrument panel affects a "gull wing" design, with divided, deeply inset faces suggestive of a modern aircraft dual cockpit. Instruments have gold pointers and numerals and are indirectly lighted to prevent glare.

Chassis is Redesigned

The frame is heavier and sturdier than ever before. Rear springs are mounted on the outside of the fully boxed side rails, 5.6 inches wider apart than on previous models. Front tread is nearly four inches wider, and the combination of wider tread and spring suspension reduces cornering roll to a minimum.

Windshield wipers are variable-speed electric; blades park off the glass when not in use.

Steering linkage is also completely new with a symmetrical idler arm design providing nearly constant ratio at all times and making steering virtually unaffected by vertical wheel action.

The brake pedal has been nearly doubled in width and is suspended from above for easier action and readier accessibility from accelerator.

Fireflite models have a new four-barrel carburetor which employs two barrels for economical cruising and all four for high speeds or a burst of acceleration. Firedome two-barrel carburetors have been redesigned for maximum efficiency.

Available optionally are: De Soto Powerflite transmission, Full-Time power steering, power brakes, four-way power seat control, electric window lifts, Airtemp air conditioning, search-tuning radio, and power operated antenna. •

1955 DE SOTO SPECIFICATIONS

Engine

	FireFlite	Firedome
Type	V-8	V-8
Bore and Stroke (in.)	3.720 x 3.44	same
Compression Ratio	7.5 to 1	same
Exhaust Valve Diameter	1.50	same
Maximum Torque (lbs. ft. at rpm)	274 at 2800	245 at 2800
Transmission	Standard	Standard
	PowerFlite	PowerFlite
	Overdrive	Overdrive

Interior Dimensions

Front Seat Width (in.)	64	same
Leg Room, Front (in.)	44	same

Capacities

Oil (quarts)		
Gasoline (gallons)	20	same
Water (quarts)	23	22
With Heater	24	23

General

Wheelbase (in.)	126	same
Overall Height (in.)	60.6	same
Overall Length (in.)	217.9	same
Overall Width (in.)	78.3	same
Tread, Front (in.)	60.22	same
Tread, Rear (in.)	59-5/8	same
Steering Ratio	nearly constant	same

DE-SOTO

with

POWER-FLITE

No work for the driver, six comfortable seats, and room to spare in Australia's first automatic car.

A milestone on the Australian motoring market is Chrysler's release of their first locally assembled cars with 12-volt ignition and automatic transmissions.

These are the Chrysler-Plymouth, the Dodge, and the De Soto. All of them are tried and proven designs which are well known and which have formed a large part of Australia's higher class motoring since the war.

The De Soto Diplomat Plaza impressed us as a sensibly-sized car with good finish and performance. It was the second car with an automatic transmission which WHEELS has tested. (The first: The Borg-Warner transmission Jaguar Mark VII, January, 1955.)

As before, the verdict is that automatic transmissions take the drudgery out of everyday driving. Automatic transmisisons are standard equipment on al but the lower priced cars in the U.S.A. and in some of the luxury cars no other transmission is available even as an optional. Of all the companies making automatic transmissions, Chrysler believe (and advertise) they have the best—Power-Flite.

Be this as it may, WHEELS found the Power-Flite equipped De Soto a revelation. The De Soto has a big, lazy slow revving engine which has obviously been designed to give a

large torque outut over its whole range. This coupled with an automatic transmission whose performance is apparently identical with a conventional clutch transmission means you have the leisures of no work combined with efficiency and economy.

The De Soto Diplomat is a fairly big car and grosses 35½ cwt. with two people and fuel; yet driven sensibly at speeds between 40 and 50 m.p.h.

on the open highway it gave better than 20 m.p.g. petrol consumption.

Its type of side-valve engine, which has given away to overhead-valve V-8 engines in the U.S.A., yet it returned nearly 15 m.p.g. during the hard and long acceleration runs as well as giving very quiet and fussless performance.

And this type of engine tops off the sense and solidity of the De

Soto design. A well-made slow-revving side-valve engine literally needs no attention whatever apart from adding oil and throwing away worn-out spark plugs. Up to 50,000 miles before lifting the head is common.

How the De Soto is made in South Australia is nearly a feature in itself. All body pressings are done there. The only imported parts are odd trim fittings such as the radiator mascot and the steering wheel.

These come from the U.S.A. along with the Power-Flite transmission. The engine is made by the British-Chrysler company which makes the British Dodge, Fargo and De Soto commercial vehicles.

Gears, including transmissions for the non-automatic cars, are Australian made.

All cars have Lucas 12-volt ignition and electrical equipment and Smiths instruments.

As such these Australian-Chrysler cars are different from their American contemporaries. They represent the latest American design modified to meet Australian requirements both to suitability and cost.

There is no clutch, just a large brake pedal and an accelerator. Transmission ranges are selected by the short steering column lever, but all forward running is done in Drive Range.

The moderate price, eye-stopping looks, and good performance of the De Soto Diplomat show that all have been satisfactorily met.

The De Soto has well-proportioned overall dimensions which allow a driver to see all four corners and make a success of parking in a narrow space.

A driver has more than good visibility without blind spots, too. The seating position is high which allows a look down at the road and the proportion of car in front and behind seems right for confident control in traffic.

The rear overhang is typical of present American car design. The boot juts out a long way past the rear wheels and is square, high, and massive. It yawns cavernously when open and swallows an unbelievable amount of luggage. It would be a safe tip that the family next door would ask you to carry the stuff they couldn't fit into their own car if you were both going holidaying at the same place. Although we are told that punctures and blow-outs are a thing of the past, you can get the spare wheel out with no trouble and without disturbing luggage.

A mild criticism is that the petrol-tank cap is placed to one side of the car and below the boot lid. The cap lies in a vertical plane and has a sharply downwards cranked filler tube. The result is that topping up is a little tricky and a goose-necked funnel would be needed for refuelling from cans.

The under-bonnet is similar to the boot in proportions. Although some of the maintainance points need a little reaching for, over the mud-guards, they can be got at with little trouble.

A tip for those used to 6-volt batteries from other American cars is that the 12-volt batteries as used in the Chrysler range need regular checking up. Their advantage (and one which U.S. manufacturers have seen since most of their cars now have them) is that they crank a big engine more easily and reliably in cold weather than a 6-volt battery.

Opening one of the De Soto's doors and stepping in is like visiting wealthy neighbours. The finish is not showy but is of good quality and everything is where you need it.

The seats are trimmed in leather. They are wide, have squabs and cushions as ample as old-fashioned arm-chairs, and are cunningly placed to give good legroom and headroom. The rear passengers still have plenty of leg room when the front seat is right back.

The appointments are sensible too. There are cigar-sized ashtrays front and rear, well placed door arm-rests which are also used as door-pulls, and the now almost forgotten rug-carrier on the back of the front seat squab.

The rear doors have adjustable quarter-pane windows which are angled back and let into the rear hood pillars. This gives wide rear access when the doors are open. The quarter-panes are well placed for ventilation and allow a good view out of the rear. The windows in the rear doors wind down fully.

The driving position is truly comfortable. The driver sits well back from the front window and facia, the steering wheel coming back on a long column to encourage relaxed seating.

Nevertheless it is not necessary to reach forward for the facia controls. They come to hand nicely. A good point about them is that they are all large and have commendably positive and obvious movements.

There are only two pedals on the floor, a large brake pedal and a fairly large floor-hinged accelerator. The front floor is as flat as is possible with leg room for everybody. The initial embarrassment of having nothing to do with the left foot and all the room in the world to put it soon wears off.

The instruments are complete. There are gauges for oil pressure, engine temperature, charge rate, and petrol. They have a well proportioned rectangular shape and flank the rectangular styled speedometer in pairs. All are easily read and have glare-free illumination at night.

The speedometer is calibrated from ten to a hundred miles-an-hour with "10" and "100" being the zero and limit points. On the test car it was somewhat out of adjustment and gave optimistic readings at its high end.

The big, six-cylinder engine starts unobtrusively and is not noticed unless it is taken to absurd high revs. The car's progression from a standing start is every bit as quiet as a town carriage.

The small steering-column selector lever for the Power-Flite transmission is worked by the left hand and its setting is recorded by a tell-tale pointer just above and behind the steering wheel hub. The positions are "L-D-N-R" which represent Low, Drive, Neutral, and Reverse Ranges.

A safety device prevents the engine being cranked in any range other than neutral.

The selector lever moves easily between Drive and Neutral but has to be lifted over stops to select Low and Reverse. There is no Parking Range as in other automatic trans-

Seats are deep and wide. Trim and upholstery is leather; the floors are carpeted. The standard of finish and the fitments are good.

The De Soto's acceleration hardly lets up to peak. The maximum speed possible in Low Range is 56 m.p.h., but shifting into Drive Range at 50 m.p.h. gave best time.

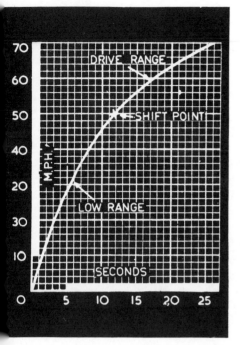

missions because the manufacturers consider their internal-expanding transmission brake, which is operated from the facia, satisfactory under all conditions.

This was borne out during the test. It pulls on quickly and then has leverage through a long travel to get maximum purchase. It pulls on with the right hand and twists anti-clockwise for release.

Drive Range is for *all* work. The Powerflite transmission has only two gears, low and drive (or 1st and top), either of which may be selected at will in Drive Range.

The low gear comes in automatically in Drive Range at speeds under 10 m.p.h. and switches out automatically to the drive gear at 56 m.ph. when full throttle acceleration is used from a standing start. The low gear can be switched in automatically under 56 m.p.h. by pressing the accelerator to the floor and tripping it past a stop.

An ingenious system of valves takes the part of the driver's mind so that the shift into and out of the low or drive gears is done on demand rather than automatically in the sense of predetermined shift points.

There is a valve on the engine, another on the tailshaft, and another on the accelerator. Thus engine speed, road speed, and throttle opening together control the transmission.

When there is a shift from one gear to the other, the take-up is nearly instantaneous. There is no apparent engine slip or lag. A wet clutch locks out the torque convertor

above 60 m.p.h. and makes the transmission "solid."

While Powerflite is as foolproof as can be it needs intelligent use for the best results.

One trap is starting the engine in Neutral (it can't be started in any other range), shifting to Drive, then revving the engine before releasing the handbrake. If this is done the De Soto will immediately, and smoothly, accelerate like a whipped horse. Those used to conventional clutches and gearboxes will be tempted to do this on hills, but it is not necessary because the De Soto will hold on anything up to a mountain pass in Drive with its engine idling.

Since there is no automatic anti-creep mechanism brought in with the foot brake when stopping the car may roll back on a steep hill. You can either leave it in Drive and balance the car with a light accelerator foot, or use the left foot on the wide brake pedal and let the engine idle in Drive. You can start by lightly pressing the accelerator and releasing the brake, or, if the hill is extremely steep and there is close traffic you can guide the car off with more acceleration and use the brake to steady it.

This left foot braking is standard practice with all automatic transmissions when parking in tight places and is the reason why the brake pedal is so wide.

We found the system wholly satisfactory, and, while different from conventional systems and so needing a readjustment of ideas, one which any driver with a little experience would pick up in a few minutes.

In most driving, including even moderately hard acceleration, the De Soto changes to Drive gear between 10 to 20 m.p.h. and its flexible engine does the rest. We got the best acceleration figures when we allowed the up-shift to occurr at 45 m.p.h. This is done by momentarily releasing the foot from the floor.

The main use for Low Range is for engine braking on steep hills. Low range may be readily selected at any speed under 56 m.p.h.

We found the De Soto's brakes were well up to the job of fast highway driving and were happily surprised that the car had engine braking which was as good as those with conventional transmissions. The brakes showed no sign of fade with normal use and stopped the car in 37 ft. from 30 m.p.h. in neutral.

We were impressed with the handling which was better at high speeds than at low speeds. The car is fitted with Oriflow shock absorbers which become progressively harder as they are worked.

At low speeds the car has a slow, easy motion to its ride and rolls sufficiently on tight corners to upset front-wheel angles if the car is pushed around hard.

The ride stiffens up at higher speeds and the suspension becomes taut and pleasant. Roll is moderate in corners and the car goes through with a slight, steadying understeer. There is negligible tyre howl at speed.

The suspension scores well on rough dirt roads because it adjusts itself to conditions. Bottoming on potholes is rare. Dust sealing both in the car and in the boot is good.

The headlights are of the well known Lucas left-hand-dipping type. They give a long, wide high beam which gives good coverage on twisty roads. It is suitable for speeds up to 70 m.p.h. The dipped beam does not trouble oncoming drivers and lights the left-hand shoulder of the road well. It is suitable for speeds up to 50 m.p.h.

TECHNICAL DETAILS
SPECIFICATION

MAKE:
De Soto Diplomat Plaza, 4-door, 6-passenger saloon; our test car from Buckle Motors (Trading Co. Pty. Ltd., Sydney.

PRICE AND AVAILABILITY:
£2,048 (incl. Sales Tax); three months.

DIMENSIONS:
Front seat: Width, 4' 8"; cushion depth, 1' 6"; squab height, 1' 8¾"; height over seat, 3' 1"; pedals to squab, 2' 11"'/3' 2"; steering wheel to squab, 11½"/1' 2½"; cushion from floor, 1' 2"; seat adjustment, 3".
Rear seat: Total width, 4' 7½"; individual width (with armrest down) 1' 11½"; cushion depth, 1' 5"; squab height, 1' 9½"; distance between seats, 10"/1' 1"; height from floor, 1' 2¾".
Doors: Front, 2' 10" x 3' 7½" (avg.); rear, 2' 6" x 3' 7½" (avg.).
Boot: 4' 2" x 3' 6½" x 1' 6" (avg. free space); spare wheel side mounted.
Overall: Wheelbase, 9' 6"; track: front 4' 7 7/8", rear 4' 10½"; length, 16' 11½"; width, 6' 1½"; height, 5' 1¾"; clearance, 7 3/8"; dry weight, 31 cwt.

ENGINE:
6-cyl. s.v., 87.31 x 114.3 mm., capacity 4,107 c.c., comp. ratio 7 to 1, 112 bhp at 3,600 rpm, 2.08 bhp/sq. in. piston area. Single downdraught carburettor with oil-bath aircleaner; full-flow oil filter. Radiator 19 pt.; sump 8 pt.; petrol tank 13 gal.

TRANSMISSION:
Power-Flite automatic transmission operated by steering column selection lever (see text); hypoid bevel final drive: ratio 3.9 to 1. Overall ratios: 3.9 to 17.43. Drive range mph: 20.4 at 1,000 rpm; 66 at 2,500 ft/min. piston speed.

CHASSIS AND BODY:
Channel-section frame; separate all-steel body.

(Continued on page 44)

DeSoto Firedome

Four-Door Sedan

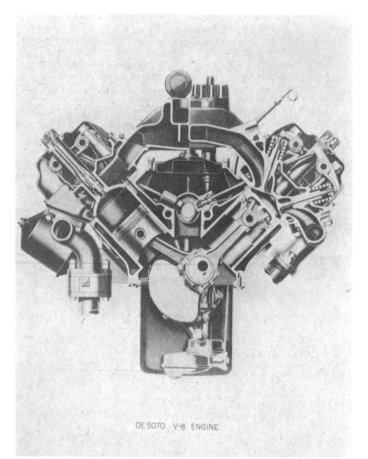

DE SOTO V-8 ENGINE

THE FIREDOME suffers from a soft suspension system whose failings are not counteracted by the new low-body design. Tendency to a roll condition can be easily encountered. Steering is reasonably positive considering the car in general, although ratio calls for too many turns of the wheel. Construction is not of the highest order and below that expected on a car of this nature. Weight, and its distribution, has much to do with the rating of this car. Engine reliability and performance are average.

the 1956 de soto

HIGHLIGHTS: top of 255 hp, four-door hardtops, pushbutton gear selector, record player

The new DeSoto convertible is three inches longer, has sportier look and has higher engine power to match its appearance.

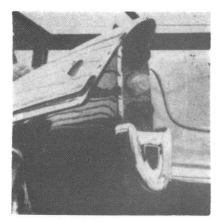

New touch: hooded tail fins over triple-lamp jet-type assembly are distinctive, give car much longer look than in 1955.

Simple front bumper has guards integral with the fine mesh grille. Side molding starts at headlight, runs to rear fins.

HEALTHY horsepower boosts and styling changes that emphasize the rakish look born in 1955 make the 1956 DeSoto point up the fact that DeSoto has undergone a complete personality switch. Up until last year, this car was noted mainly for its comfort, dependability and sound engineering. Performance and styling, both very conservative, had never been strong selling points. It appears now that DeSoto hopes to increase its buyer appeal by adding improvements in both these departments to its more traditional attractions.

Both the Firedome and Fireflite engines, at 291 inches in '55, now displace 330 cubic inches. The Firedome is rated at 230 hp (up from 185) and delivers 305 foot-pounds of torque at 2800 rpm. The Firedome has been raised from 200 to 255 hp and from 274 to 350 foot-pounds of torque at 3200 rpm—more than last year's Chrysler New Yorker! Both engines are slightly under square with bore of 3.72 inches and stroke of 3.80 inches. A two-barrel carb is used on the Firedome; a four-barrel on the Fireflite. Dual exhausts can be had with both engines.

As might be expected, the added power showed up in a noticeable improvement in performance during a pre-introduction trial ride. Since the '55 models were no slouches (the '55 Fireflite turned 0 to 60 in an average of 12.5 seconds during MOTOR LIFE's road test), the new models will likely be able to hold their own in any league. The increase in the stroke by nearly half an inch should show up particularly well in the lower speed range and traffic light tussles.

Stylingwise big things have happened also. DeSoto has finally lost its toothy grin. A fine mesh-like grille has replaced the horizontal bar and "teeth" arrangement, a DeSoto trademark.

Rear fender lines now sweep up, giving the wedge-shaped effect evident in all Chrysler Corporation cars this year. Body side molding accentuates this upswept look. Tail light assemblies have been completely redesigned, now have brow formed by tip of rear fender.

Four-door hardtops are now offered in both the Firedome and Fireflite series.

Push-button gearshift arrangement is standard on all DeSotos equipped with PowerFlite transmissions. The Highway Hi-Fi record player is available as an option along with the usual array of power-assist items and other accessories.

Interiors are similar to last year, retaining the unique twin-cowl instrument panel. Interior trim and upholstery remains very attractive, with enough combinations available to suit almost any buyer.

Riding qualities offer the traditional DeSoto comfort. Seat design is excellent and, though springing is relatively soft, the Oriflow shocks and wide rear spring mounting help keep the car from excessive sway in cornering under all normal conditions. No small car, the DeSoto can't be thrown around like one, but its handling should be more than equal to the demands of most drivers.

DeSoto sales climbed tremendously after the 1955 models were introduced. The new models look to be a cinch to consolidate these gains and even extend them further. •

1956 De Soto

FIREFLITE SPORTSMAN

THE two DeSotos for 1956, Firedome and FireFlite, are classic examples of inter-company competition. The two DeSotos, differing only in trim, engine horsepower and torque (Firedome has two-barrel carburetor, develops 230 bhp; FireFlite has four-barrels and 255 bhp), straddle the 225 bhp Chrysler Windsor price-wise.

Firedome four-door sedan is approximately $200 less than the equivalent model Windsor, while the FireFlite costs $100-plus more. All three share the same body shells and 126-inch wheelbase chassis; weights of the sedans are all within a 100-lb. spread.

What it all adds up to is that the DeSoto Firedome is a really outstanding value package. It has the exceptionally roomy Chrysler senior body shell with a tremendous trunk and the soft surface and firm support of Chrysler Corporation's excellent foam upholstery. Although the weight of the car is about 400 lbs. more than the smaller Dodge, the engine produces the same horsepower without four-barrel carburetion or extra-cost power-boosting equipment.

Both DeSotos share a remarkable combination of comfort and roadability. In this respect we feel that DeSoto *excels* all other Chrysler products in this important quality. (Note: Chrysler Windsor has not been tested at press time.) Last year's DeSotos had the same superior riding comfort but had tendencies to excessive brake dive, a somewhat "soft" feel in the front end and too much "lean" in curves. Some minor engineering changes have ironed out these problems for the most part. A newly-designed torsion bar stabilizer on the front suspension and an additional rear spring-leaf have greatly increased firmness and stability.

Weight distribution helps too. The 126-inch wheelbase chassis and senior Chrysler body permit the compact hemispherical combustion chambered engine to be placed just to the rear of the front axle line instead of over it. The result is that the big softly-sprung car hangs on like a leëch in sharp curves. On a sharply winding loose dirt road it takes a deliberate effort to put the car into a rear-wheel drift.

With the tremendous torque available, (CAR LIFE's test car was a 255 bhp FireFlite), a quick jab on the throttle and a slight correction of the wheel will snap the car back on the track instantly. The soft springs permit considerable lean in maneuvers like this, but the suspension and chassis balance, to give the driver a feeling of control and stability throughout.

The springing and Oriflow shock absorbers control pitching and rebound almost completely. The car is wonderfully smooth and steady over high-crowned, twisting blacktop roads at high speeds. At the same time surface irregularities are blotted up so that they can hardly be felt. In this last respect the DeSoto was superior to the Chrysler New Yorker.

One slight flaw in the control set-up is the rather high ratio of power steering which tends to reduce the feel of the road. In other words, a small movement of the wheel rim results in an indefinite response of the car's directional control.

Power-wise the DeSoto PowerFlite engine leaves very little to be desired, with an 0 to 60 time of 11.5 seconds and quick response in the higher speed ranges.

Styling is considerably improved for 1956. The color sweep down the side panels follows the uplifted rear fender fins and balances the car's overall appearance. Color combinations, both upholstery and paint, may be a bit flamboyant for your taste. Better *see* the effect of the color combination you desire before placing an order. The mesh grille is a pleasing change from the familiar chrome-plated "teeth" of past years.

Summing up: If you like the styling, DeSoto may well be the top value for those who want a larger, roomier car than the low and low-medium price ranges have to offer. DeSoto is a really big car without any of the hard-to-handle awkwardness common to the size and weight. Parking is a cinch if the space is big enough! For an all-around combination of size, performance, sheer comfort and roadability, DeSoto's equal is hard to find. ●

PERFORMANCE ☑ ☑ ☑ ☑ ☐

Fireflite's four-barrel carburetor and 255 bhp puts it right at the head of its class. The two-barrel carburetor on the Firedome version limits output to 230 bhp. This power gives acceleration at high speeds without need for down-shifting.

STYLING ☑ ☑ ☑ ☑ ☐

Grille is simpler, neater this year. Color sweep on the sides and rear quarter panel has been greatly improved. Some color combinations are pleasing, others seem a bit gaudy. General effect is pleasing.

RIDING COMFORT ☑ ☑ ☑ ☑ ☑

Leads all others in its class except its sister car, Chrysler Windsor, helped by a nearly perfect combination of suspension elements that control sway, and all but eliminate rebound and pitching. Tires, springs and upholstery are soft enough to minimize surface jarring.

INTERIOR DESIGN ☑ ☑ ☑ ☑ ☐

Seats and seating position are excellent. Upholstery is deep yet firm. Wheel position and vision is good. Plenty of back seat leg room even in hardtop coupes. Instruments and controls are well placed; however, white and gold dials are difficult to read at night.

ROADABILITY ☑ ☑ ☑ ☑ ☐

Very good, considering the smooth soft ride that the suspension provides. New front stabilizer has considerably reduced roll and sway on curves. Car is very stable at high speeds and good on high crowned twisting roads.

EASE OF CONTROL ☑ ☑ ☑ ☑ ☐

Power steering, necessary on a car of DeSoto's size, lacked precision and road sense on CAR LIFE'S test DeSoto. Newly-designed brakes with power assist are smooth and positive, free from grabbing action. Pushbutton transmission control is effortless and convenient.

ECONOMY ☑ ☑ ☑ ☑ ☐

Not a first consideration on a 4,000-lb. car, yet the Fireflite gives about 15.5 mpg. at 50 mph. This, in a heavy car capable of 0 to 60 mph in 11.5 seconds, indicates good engineering. Firedome engine of 230 bhp is available with overdrive and should be most economical.

SERVICEABILITY ☑ ☑ ☑ ☑ ☐

Hemispherical combustion chamber, on both Fireflite and Firedome engines, requires spark plugs buried in the valve rocker covers. Other engine components are readily accessible. Chassis is well-designed and easy to work on.

WORKMANSHIP ☑ ☑ ☑ ☑ ☐

On par with cars in its price class but not the top of the group. Tailoring of seats, rugs and door panels is good, but fitting is faulty on window sill panels and interior metal trim. On the plus side: windows and windshield of hardtop were absolutely rattle free.

DURABILITY ☑ ☑ ☑ ☑ ☑

DeSoto's construction is very sound. Body is solid and rattle free. Engine is Chrysler's original Firepower design, one of the best ever put in production. Power-Flite transmission has an excellent freedom-from-repair record. Car is obviously built to last.

VALUE PER DOLLAR ☑ ☑ ☑ ☑ ☑

Although not a cheap car, DeSoto, with Chrysler's largest body shell, a powerful dependable engine, excellent roadability and outstanding riding comfort, represents a tremendous amount of luxury transportation value at the price.

FIREFLITE

DESOTO IS THE CAR FOR YOU

If . . . You are looking for a car that rates at the top of the ride-comfort list on *all* U.S. automobiles plus excellent roadability.

If . . . You want an extremely roomy car with lots of luggage space and a comfortable and quiet interior comparable to the top luxury cars in everything but detail and trim.

If . . . You want a car that's colorful, stylish and sporty, yet dependable and completely practical.

If . . . You want fairly "hot" performance from an engine and transmission of proved dependability in a medium-heavy car, and are willing to forego high gasoline mileage.

If . . . You want a car almost as big as the top luxury group yet one that is a pleasure to park and easy to drive in traffic.

DRIVER'S REPORT

DESOTO FIREFLITE

*This one, quite literally, has everything—
from Hi-Fi and air conditioning
to wheel spinning acceleration*

BY JACK CORTINE

Air conditioning unit in trunk includes
two controls for admitting fresh air
that are closed only in dust and cold.

Hi-Fi player does not interfere with foot room. Records may be carried inside unit, but glove compartment seems easier.

Records are special 16⅔ rpm, although trade sources say this speed soon will be used by standard non-portable machines.

Outlet for cold air is on package shelf, works fine, but when three ride in back seat, man in middle gets a strong draft.

DE SOTO isn't the car it used to be. Not so long ago it was a rather quiet and sedate type of family car that had its faithful. Last year, however, it broke rather drastically with the conservative past—and the current 1956 model now stands as about as hot and jazzy piece of machinery as you can find out of Detroit.

We drove the 255-hp Fireflite version for about 10 days and found it to be unusually interesting. Some of this was due to the fact that the four-door sedan was equipped with air conditioning and the already famous "Highway Hi-Fi" record player. But no less notable was the remarkable increase in accelerating ability.

It was only a little more than nine months ago that we assisted in road testing the 1955 DeSoto. It is worth repeating the times recorded then: 0-30 mph in 4.5 seconds, 0-45 in 8.4 and 0-60 in 12.5. Now hear this.

The 1956 version we've just finished driving cranked out a really hot 3.8 seconds from 0-30 mph, 6.2 seconds from 0-45 mph and 9.3 seconds from a standing start to 60 mph. All these are actual times obtained with a calibrated speedometer. As a matter of fact, we had a little trouble getting a solid bite on the pavement with the rear tires, since the tendency to spin the rear wheels was frequent.

The speedo deserves a bit of comment. It was the most accurate yet checked on a standard passenger 1956 car. Up to 55 mph, it was right on the nose, then gained about one mph for each additional five until, at 106 mph, it was registering 117 mph.

Very briefly, the source of the quicker characteristics of the 1956 Fireflite is not hard to find. Right under the hood are 330 cubic inches, 39 more than there were last year. And you know the old saying

about trying to find a substitute for 'em. Compression ratio, too, is up a full notch, from 7.5 to 8.5-to-1. Most of the other engine refinements are secondary in importance. But it's interesting that crankcase oil capacity has been reduced from five quarts to four.

The one department where all these engine improvements apparently have been for naught is in gas mileage. Last year it recorded an average of 17.5 to 20 mpg at various speeds. This year's car batted an average of 15 mpg for all driving—city, country and testing.

On the control side, it is amazing how the engineers for DeSoto have wrought the miracle of building in even better handling on so hefty a car. Power steering ratios, of course, are quicker, but the ride around bends is flatter and surer than ever. Improvements continued at this rate will one day enable standard sedans to skate through corners as nimbly as a sportster.

Announcement of the record-player unit was accompanied by some jeering laughs and "what'll they try next?" But, take my word for it, the outfit (not a true hi-fi) is really worth more than the $75 extra. It's a solid improvement in riding pleasure, especially if you can't take too many of those irritating commercials as the penalty for radio listening. The record selection (special 16⅔ rpm) is wide, plenty more are available, and the mechanism is positively foolproof. The hardest bounce the DeSoto could take without going on its head failed to move the needle a single groove on the wax.

Each record plays about 40 minutes to a side and changing takes only a few seconds at a stoplight. The layout is compact and out of the way.

The air conditioner has two tempera-

ture levels (cold and cool) and runs off a two-speed blower. Interior air is exhausted by two intakes flanking the blower outlet and the entire setup works nicely, except for one feature: if three passengers ride in the rear seat, the man in the middle gets the frigid draft right in the back of his head.

A lot of people have been going for the DeSoto, as booming sales figures prove. You'll be hearing much more about it as an obviously new policy of pushing for the discriminating buyer supplants the old family appeal line. The DeSoto got new styling last year; now it boasts acceleration and gadgets to make the package complete. •

Engine compartment with air conditioning is loaded to capacity. Interesting sidelight: DeSoto had no under-hood sound pad, yet engine noise was slight.

'56 DE SOTO ROAD TEST

...Shows why this car, 11th in sales in '55, has become an even bigger seller this model year

AN MT RESEARCH REPORT

DESOTO SALES tell a story that conforms nicely to some of our conclusions on the "Why buy a DeSoto?" question. Sympathetic critics might say that DeSoto has seemed destined to play a somewhat subdued role, often overshadowed by fast-selling Plymouths, chrome-and-color Dodges, or Chrysler power. But a turning point came in '55, when DeSoto dropped its once-venerable, now-vulnerable 6-cylinder engine, took on "Forward Look" style, a competitive power boost, and gave sales a shakeup.

Here's what happened: Plymouth went from 5th place in '54 to 4th in '55; Dodge held fast to hotly-contested 8th place, and Chrysler moved up one important slot to take over 9th place in '55. But DeSoto came up with some earned runs to move from 13th place to 11th to gain the most-improved-player award on a vastly improved team. And our '56 test car revealed why this should be another successful year.

Test car: Fireflite "Sportsman" 2-door hardtop, equipped with power steering, power brakes, electric window lifts, deluxe radio, hot-water heater, special leather upholstery. PowerFlite automatic transmission is standard on all Fireflites.

EASE OF DRIVING

Power-assisted or standard-steering DeSotos rate praise, particularly when the going gets rough; steering wheel fight from front-wheel movement is at a minimum. The biggest difference between the 2 steering systems is found in the number of steering wheel turns needed to move the wheels when turning corners or in parking; mechanical systems require 5½ turns lock-to-lock, while power steering only needs 3½. Power-boosted turns can be made more easily and quickly, but it's difficult to move the wheels with power off even when the car is moving slowly.

DeSotos are large cars and there will be some places where the car just won't fit, even tho the upswept rear fenders serve as guides to the car's length and width and the steering is so easy. To some people, there's a drawback to this absence of effort: lack of road feel. We find early in Chrysler-product tests with power steering that you must learn to compensate for overcorrecting in turns. You have to feel your way thru tight turns a little more carefully than with other cars, for front-end wander or steering disturbances aren't transmitted to you until you're moving across the white line in a drift. On the straights you make numerous fingertip corrections for crosswinds; uneven road crowns or dips.

If you're tall you may have to lower your head slightly when you 1st look thru the windshield because of the combination of high seat and fairly low roofline. We didn't find much distortion at the outer edges of the windshield, tho we contend that *any* is too much to sacrifice for the sake of styling. The windshield wiper sweep was poor at the sides (see accompanying photo), while the upswept area at the center was magnified by the reduced height of the windshield.

One of the most important assets to ease of driving is a legible instrument panel. In our estimation the DeSoto panel is near tops in esthetic appeal. The instruments themselves are possibly too delicate in that they don't telegraph their message instantly. They need better contrast between needles, numbers and background.

Glareproofing of the panel is handled efficiently by flat paint in the event you don't wish the optional padding with its definitely richer look. For trips the true map-reading light (missing from many new cars) beneath each cowl of the panel is a desirable feature. You'll find a difference in control placement dependent on whether or not the car has PowerFlite, is a Fireflite or Firedome; regardless of individual placement, all are within reach.

Described after our 1st tryout as "more than just a gimmick," pushbutton shifting *can* be genuinely desirable. But it takes more than intermittent driving to fully appreciate or become used to it. You'll like some of the features incorporated into its design: Stabbing at the panel in an emergency slow-down situation during the test we inadvertently poked a finger at the REVERSE button instead of LOW; rather than strewing pieces of PowerFlite along the road, the car simply coasted in neutral —undesirable under the circumstances, but far better than a costly transmission replacement or repair job. The gearbox had been saved by the fact that at speeds over 10 mph, reverse is blocked out automatically. Another good feature was incorporated early this year; a button now stays pushed in as long as the car is in gear. On pre-January models, touching any button

40

the wheels track well, the rear end stays put; even under hard driving conditions, roadability qualities offer a generous margin for error.

These qualities are a result of '55 refinements: repositioned Oriflow shock absorbers (front shocks are within the coil springs, rear shocks are sea-leg mounted), stiffer frame, rear springs some 5 inches farther apart than in '54; front tread was widened by 4 inches last year to eliminate much of the cornering mushiness and instability common to the older cars. This year, Fireflites have 6 leaves in their rear springs, Firedomes have 4; station wagon has wider front and rear tread than coupes and sedans, uses 7-leaf rear springs.

RIDE

It's possible that as many DeSotos are bought for their good ride traits as for any other factor. It's always been a comfortable, roomy car. At high speeds, the car

surprise at the general spaciousness of the coupe. Legroom is foreshortened some 3 inches compared to a 4-door sedan, but very reasonable for a coupe with the front-seat legroom (an inch greater than sedan's) offered in this car. Headroom is a mere half-inch less than in a sedan.

ACCELERATION

Added engine displacement means another model-year improvement in DeSoto passing prowess, and as in the past, it's come about without added engine noise or harsh downshift snap. Here's a brief on what DeSoto engineers have done for highway-speed passing safety in the few years this factor has been a selling point: In '53, MT's tests showed a DeSoto (with Fluid-Torque transmission) capable of going from 50 to 80 mph in 25.4 seconds; in '54 our DeSoto test car moved thru the same speeds in about 19 seconds. Last year, 50-80 times were faster again by

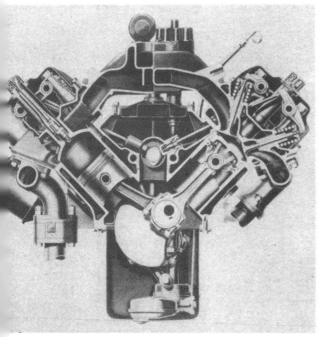

Cutaway view of DeSoto's 255-hp V8 shows compact arrangement of components. Single camshaft in center operates valves thru a series of hydraulic tappets, push-rods, and rocker arms. Note the efficient location of valves and air passages

COLIN CREITZ

With the aircleaner removed, Firedome's relatively minute carburetor becomes apparent. Sparkplugs are concealed beneath the stamped valve covers for protection from dirt and water. Round object at top is part of power brake system

(without pushing hard enough to put it in gear) could make all the buttons pop out, creating the possibility of the car remaining in gear without your knowing it.

An added improvement would be in nighttime lighting; at present all buttons glow with equal brightness, and a glance isn't enough to tell what gear is engaged.

ROADABILITY

With a chassis largely unchanged for 56, the DeSoto retains the feeling of unwanted front-end movement in hard cornering, but it's largely body movement, for

wanders very little; wind noise, with vents open or closed, is low; road noise is well controlled.

As a passenger in the front seat of the DeSoto, you have nothing to do but sit back, stretch your legs as far as you like, and relax. There is no padding on the panel in front of you, but no injury-causing accessories or obstructions, either.

Long noted for spacious sedan dimensions, DeSoto carries its reputation to the hardtops; although hiproom is compressed to 55 inches (sedans measure 64 inches in width) our rear seat passengers expressed

nearly 5 seconds, and this year the time was cut even further.

A passing-gear kickdown (to LOW gear) was possible up to a true 50 mph in the test car; a manual shift, a la pushbutton, could be made at higher speeds, but with no gain in power, regardless of the added rpms it wrung out of the engine. At times, what felt like another kickdown was actually the 2nd pair of carburetor barrels cutting in under part-throttle vacuum drop. But this kick-in-the-pants shot of fuel mixture hitting the cylinders indicated inefficient carburetion, for the en-

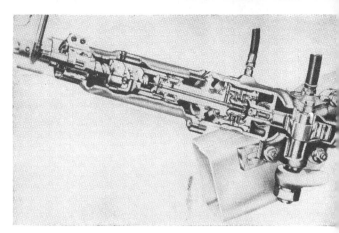

Hydraulic pressure for actuating the full-time coaxial power steering unit is derived from a generator driven pump (above). A broken fan belt would naturally result in a loss of power. A hydraulic ram operates the rack and pinion gear in the steering unit itself. An oil cushion between the steering wheel actuated valve and the ram insulates any feeling of the road from the driver. On hydraulic failure, the ram cylinder collapses and the system continues to function mechanically

gine shouldn't have been screaming for this added charge at cruising speeds. Instead of a smooth, nearly unnoticed transition from 2- to 4-barrel carburetion, we had only a lugging feeling moving up grades at 50-60 mph before the sudden cut-in. Common causes of this condition could be improper fuel mixture (too lean), sticking float valve, or maladjusted vacuum control lever. Investigation revealed that it was the latter.

Transmission changes: Standing-start acceleration benefits from a change in torque converter specifications. The stator blade angle of the impeller element (in the Fireflite's transmission only) has been altered to give what DeSoto engineers refer to as a 90-90 PowerFlite transmission. (The figure—formerly 90-80—refers to the angle at which the oil enters and leaves the turbine.) The result is a higher converter stall-torque point, a slightly higher torque multiplication factor. Now, when you hold the brake on, floor the throttle, the engine tachometer reads some 300 rpm higher than it did on a '55 Fireflite or on a '56 Firedome; letting the engine speed up a little more as you start off promotes peppier pickup from a standstill.

Transmissions in the 2 models are otherwise similar to '55, and mechanically similar to each other. A big difference, tho, is in cooling systems. Fireflite automatics are water-cooled, Firedome PowerFlites are air-cooled. (With more powerful, higher-revving engines speeding up the transmissions, an overheating problem can arise; DeSoto is playing it safe, beating trouble to the punch with this liquid cooling system. But we feel that even a Firedome in severe use should show no converter weakness, for we've found from our tests that it takes unusual punishment to produce overheated-oil conditions in PowerFlites.

Engine changes: Prime changes from last year's 200-bhp version include a compression ratio increase to 8.5 to 1 (was 7.5), and a stroking job which brought displacement up from 291 to 330.4 cubic inches.

Bore is unchanged; intake and exhaust valves are larger, intake ports are redesigned for big-engine breathing efficiency.

DeSoto's 255-horsepower V8 is one of the few hemispherical-combustion-chamber engines on our market. Costlier to produce than conventional types, this double-rocker-arm, overhead-valve V8's design is found only in the DeSoto Firedome and Chrysler New Yorker.

Ignition supplier Auto-Lite has provided what could be an added boon to DeSoto engine efficiency with the "Power Tip" sparkplug. This long-reach plug, designed basically for '56 Chrysler-product V8s (but now available for all late-model engines except L-head types), puts its firing tip further into the combustion chamber for more even, more complete mixture burning. And it's a turn-about proposition, for being in the thick of things, the plug benefits from the scouring action of the gases on exhaust strokes.

Because it burns hotter at low speeds, the plug is supposed to do a better clean-up job on carbon and oil deposits; taking advantage of the refrigerating action of rich, high-speed fuel mixtures, the plug burns cooler at wide-open throttle.

BRAKING

We'll bet that you inadvertently set your left foot on the brake pedal. It's easy to do this, whether you're just parked, or looking for a way to slow down in a hurry. Like other Chrysler Corp. suspended power brake pedals, DeSoto's is extra-wide, higher than some power pedals, but still in a good spot for pivoting from accelerator to brake on your right heel.

Altho always good stoppers, some of our DeSoto test cars have been prone to brake fade without too much provocation; thus we were anxious to find out if the new center-plane brakes (installed on both De-Sotos and both Chryslers; March MT) would alleviate this condition as claimed. The new brakes are a definite improvement, coming thru our trying 12-successive-stops fade tests with good results, by comparison to the former brake system.

Uneven brake pull during or following the test was moderate; brakes returned to normal in a remarkably short time. (See table on opposite page for details.)

FUEL ECONOMY

Test car's highway and in-town averages (figures shown are corrected to odometer error) should be a good mark for tank-checkers to shoot at, for while they may seem low to some drivers, they're pretty good to those people suffering from gasbillitis. Looking at the steady-speed fuel economy figures, comparative standards showing the car's capabilities, you'll see a commendable showing, considering the engine displacement increase. Economy increase notwithstanding, you may go farther on a tankful in a '56, for the gas tank is a gallon larger!

All tests were run using Mobilgas Special, for premium-grade gas is recommended in the Fireflite engine; Firedomes, according to DeSoto sources, *can* be operated on regular-grade gas, if proper timing adjustment is made when the car is tuned.

GETTING IN AND OUT

Last year's doorhandles drew complaint from MT (and many DeSoto owners) because they offered such a poor leverage device for gripping the handle. The handle was integral with a pushbutton; when the thumb-sized button was pushed, the handle popped out. The cries were heard, for this year there's a convenient button-and-handle setup that can't be criticized.

When getting into our DeSoto hardtop test car we didn't come close to the wraparound section of the door jamb, tho we unconsciously ducked beneath the one-inch-lower roofline. Holding open the heavier door of 2-doors becomes a problem only to rear-seat passengers who have to slip between the seatback and rear door frame to settle into the roomy back seat. There's a noticeable difference between the DeSoto's dimensions and those of the "popular priced" hardtops. Our test car carried optional seatbelts, but there were no rear-floor (*continued on page* 44)

PERFORMANCE

'56

(255-bhp engine)

'55

(200-bhp engine)

	'56	'55
ACCELERATION	From Standing Start 0-30 mph 4.0 0-60 mph 10.9 Quarter-mile 17.8 and 78.5 mph	From Standing Start 0-30 mph 4.3 0-60 mph 12.8 Quarter-mile 19.2 and 76 mph
	Passing Speeds 30-50 mph 3.9 50-80 mph 11.2	Passing Speeds 30-50 mph 4.9 50-80 mph 14.3
FUEL CONSUMPTION	Used Mobilgas Special Stop-and-Go Driving 12.8 mpg highway trip average 11.1 mpg city driving average 13.8 mpg over measured course 12.6 mpg tank average for 580 miles	Used Mobilgas Regular Stop-and-Go Driving 12.4 mpg over measured course 12.2 mpg tank average for 613 miles
	Steady Speeds 19.6 mpg @ 30 17.8 mpg @ 45 15.3 mpg @ 60 12.5 mpg @ 75	Steady Speeds 19.7 mpg @ 30 18.2 mpg @ 45 15.7 mpg @ 60 11.9 mpg @ 75
STOPPING DISTANCE	145 feet from 60 mph	146 feet from 60 mph
BRAKE FADE	Slight on 4th stop from 60 Complete after 9th stop Complete recovery 3 minutes	
TOP SPEED	Fastest run 111.4 Slowest 106.2 Average of 4 runs 108.7	Fastest run 106 Slowest 101.1 Average of 4 runs 103.2
SPEEDOMETER ERROR	Read 33 at true 30, 49 at 45 66 at 60, and 82 at 75	Read 32 at true 30, 48 at 45 63 at 60, and 79 at 75

'56 DE SOTO

Fireflite 2-door hardtop with PowerFlite

SPECIFICATIONS

ENGINE: Ohv V8. Bore 3.72 in. Stroke 3.80 in. Stroke/bore ratio 1.02:1. Compression ratio 8.5:1. Displacement 330.4 cu. in. Advertised bhp 255 @ 4400 rpm. Bhp per cu. in. 0.771. Piston travel @ max. bhp 2786 ft. per min. Max. bmep 159.7 psi. Max. torque 350 lbs.-ft. @ 3200 rpm.

TRANSMISSION: Standard transmission is PowerFlite, 3-element torque converter using planetary gears. Overdrive transmission not available on Fireflite models.

REAR-AXLE RATIOS: PowerFlite 3.54.

STEERING: Number of turns lock to lock 3½ (power steering).

WEIGHT: Test car weight (with gas, oil, and water) 4397. Test car weight/bhp ratio 17.2:1.

TIRES: 7.60 x 15 tubeless.

PRICES: (Including suggested retail price at main factory, federal tax, and delivery and handling charges, but not freight.) FIREDOME 4-door sedan $2632, 2-door hardtops $2688 and $2809, 4-door hardtops $2787 and $2908, convertible $3036, 4-door station wagon $3325.

FIREFLITE 4-door sedan $3074, 2-door hardtop $3301, 4-door hardtop $3386, convertibles $3499 and $3570. ADVENTURER 2-door hardtop $3683.

ACCESSORIES: PowerFlite standard equipment, power brakes $40, power steering $97, power windows $102, 4-way power seat $70, radios $98 and $119, heaters $82 and $129, air conditioning $427 and $567.

DIMENSIONS

A FRONT OVERHANG **36.6**
B WHEELBASE **126**
C REAR OVERHANG **55.3**
D OVERALL HEIGHT **62.7** (**60.6** loaded)
E MINIMUM GROUND CLEARANCE **6.2**
    (at frame sidemember)
F FRONT LEGROOM **45.7**
G REAR LEGROOM **44.7**

H FRONT HEADROOM **35.1**
I REAR HEADROOM **34.5**
J OVERALL LENGTH **217.9**
K OVERALL WIDTH **78.3**
L FRONT SHOULDER ROOM **58.4**
M REAR SHOULDER ROOM **58.4**
N TRUNK CAPACITY **N/A**

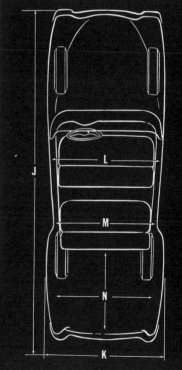

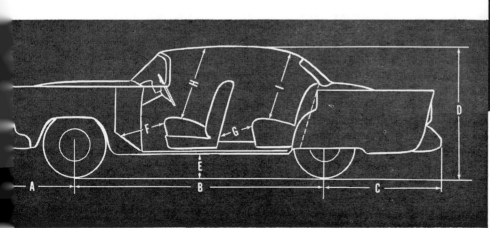

continued from page 42

DeSoto Road Test

belt-attachment plates to trip us up or take up valuable floor space as in most installations. In the DeSoto, the belts loop around a special seat-frame bar; the bar is then connected thru the floorboard to a frame crossmember via steel cable running unseen beneath the rear floormat.

HOW WELL IT'S CONSTRUCTED

Looking the test car over carefully, we found some common ailments—orange-peel marring the paint, misaligned inner windshield molding and doorsills. We found no traces of equally-common body-joint file marks or misfitted upholstery. No water leaks thru doors or windows; no moisture in huge trunk even after snow had piled up on decklid for 3 days. Chrome-pitting may soon be a thing of the past; DeSoto makes extensive use of aluminum in grille, uses anodizing method to give Adventurer gold trim. We encountered no troubles whatsoever during the test. Transmission operated smoothly and quietly, drive train had no whines or vibrations. Engine condition normal at all times; cold-morning warmup time was about par for the big V8 course.

SERVICING

Mechanics have had plenty of experience with this Chrysler-based V8, should effect efficient repairs when necessary. If there's anything unusual about repairs, maintenance or longevity, MT usually learns about it. DeSotos, on this basis, are apparently giving reliable service, for we've heard nothing to the contrary.

OTHER OPTIONS

DeSoto buyers can get 2 air conditioners (recirculating and fresh-air types), a gasoline-fired, extra-hot heater, a "Highway Hi-Fi" record player, even a $39, 15-jewel, self-winding watch mounted in the steering wheel hub. Bodies come in 14 solids, about 84 2-tones, with multi-colored interiors fashioned in nylon-faced brocade material, all-vinyl or all-leather upholstery. PowerFlite and overdrive transmissions are extra-cost in the Firedome series, cost $179 and $107, respectively; dealers have a not-too-wide range of interchangeable axle ratios, but enough to meet most normal driving needs. Our test car was equipped with the standard 3.54 ratio, satisfactory for economy-acceleration requirements during the test.

OTHER MODELS

Don't let anyone refer to the less-expensive DeSoto Firedome as the "small" DeSoto. Inch-for-inch, its body and engine are every bit as big as the Fireflite. Powerwise, it mounts a 2-barrel carburetor instead of a 4-barrel model, has a milder camshaft, puts out 25 less horsepower. Appearance-wise it's easily mistaken for a Fireflite, for it differs only in headlight rim styling, lack of fender-top chrome, top quarter-panel trim, and in fender nameplate script. Firedome interiors are less fancy, but tasteful.

Latest model option is the Adventurer (see March MT), a special gold-hued 2-door hardtop with a 320-horsepower engine. Power isn't its only distinction; its chassis is stiffer for safety and durability.

Counting both series, there are a pair of 4-door sedans, 4 2-door hardtops, and 3 4-door hardtops, 3 convertibles (Firedome, Fireflite and specially trimmed "Pace Car" model), and, in the Firedome series only, a handsome station wagon.

SUMMING UP

Stylish, colorful, lively, up-to-date in every selling respect. That sounds basically like a pretty good outline for marketing in any price class, and sounds familiarly like the new DeSoto. Intensive advertising, spotlighted ventures like pacing the '56 Indianapolis "500," and introduction of "specials" like the Adventurer keep De Soto in the public's mind more than ever before.

Some models call for a good-sized down payment, but keep in mind that there's a spread in price, from the Firedome sedan to the deluxe Adventurer, of over $1000.
—Jim Lodge

DE SOTO, WITH POWER-FLITE

(Continued from page 33)

SUSPENSION:
I.f.s. by coil and wishbones, rear by semi-elliptic leaf; telescopic *Oriflow* shock absorbers.

BRAKES:
4-wheel hydraulic; mechanical hand linkage to internal-expanding transmission brake from facia mounted lever. Friction lining area 158 sq. in. Ratios: 117 sq. in. per unladen ton; 89 sq. in. per laden ton.

STEERING:
Worm and two-tooth roller; 3 7/8 turns from lock to lock; turning circle 39 ft.

ELECTRICAL EQUIPMENT:
12-volt ignition, 36/42-watt headlamps, dual horns, dual wipers, automatic courtesy light.

WHEELS AND TYRES:
Pressed steel discs with 5-stud attachment; 6.70-15 tyres; recommended pressures 24 lb. per sq. in. front and rear.

PERFORMANCE

TOP SPEED:
Average of test runs .... 80.4 mph
Fastest one way .... 82.5 mph

MAXIMUM SPEED ON GEARS:
Low range, 56 mph; *recommended shift points,* see text.

ACCELERATION:
Standing ¼-mile: Average of test runs, 21.23 sec.; fastest one way, 21.2 sec.
Acceleration through gears: 0-10 mph, 1.5 sec.; 0.20 mph, 3.2 sec.; 0-30 mph, 5.3 sec.; 0-40 mph, 8.1 sec.; 0-50 mph, 11.8 sec.; 0-60 mph, 17.1 sec.; 0.70 mph, 26.0 sec.
Acceleration in gears—Low Range: 20-30 mph, 3.1 sec.; 20-40 mph, 4.9 sec.; 20-50 mph, 7.6 sec.; *Drive Range:* 20-30 mph, 3.5 sec.; 20-40 mph, 7.1 sec.; 20-50 mph, 10.4 sec.; 20-60 mph, 15.5 sec.; 20-70 mph, 24.5 sec.

Drive Range acceleration: 30-50 mph, 8.8 sec.; 40-60 mph, 9.9 sec.; 50-70 mph, 11.0 sec.

BEST HILL CLIMBING:
Drive range: 1 in 4.17 at constant 30 mph.
Low range: 1 in 2 at constant 22 mph.

BRAKING:
Footbrake at 30 mph in neutral, 37 ft.
Handbrake at 30 mph in neutral, 121 ft.
Fade (see text) nil with fast highway driving.

SPEEDO ERROR:
20 mph (indicated)—19.6 mph (actual); 30 mph—29 mph; 40 mph—38.2 mph; 50 mph—46.4 mph; 60 mph—56.2 mph; 70 mph—65.3 mph; 80 mph—73.7 mph.

TEST WEIGHT:
Driver, assistant, full tank, and gear: 35½ cwt.
Distribution: front 19 cwt; rear 16½ cwt.

PETROL CONSUMPTION:
Hard driving, 14.6 mpg; normal highway cruising, 20.9 mpg. Fuel used: pump petrol.

BY RACER BROWN

RODDERS TEST INDY PACE CAR

To the victor belongs the spoils!" In this case, the victor is the "handler" who can out-handle the field, whose pit crew and car are the sharpest and who is possessed of the degree of stamina necessary to win the 1956 Indianapolis 500 mile race on Memorial Day. We wouldn't dare predict a winner, but whoever the lucky guy is, the loot, or at least a good share of it, is represented in this month's test car, the '56 DeSoto convertible pace car.

Everyone acquainted with the race knows the duty of the pace car; lead the 33-car starting field around the track for a lap or two, mash the throttle on the last turn leading to the starting flag, then duck along the pit wall before being trampled into the bricks by the screaming pack. This year's pace car is blessed with the power to escape unscathed, but I wouldn't want to race the Offies into the first turn with it. This isn't throwing rocks at the DeSoto because, let's face it, it's a stock '56 production convertible with a gold and white paint job and trim to set it apart from others.

Our test of the actual pace car was necessarily brief, as will be our report. The car was a "Fireflite" convertible equipped with PowerFlite, power steering, power brakes, a power-operated top, deluxe radio, "Hiway Hi-Fi" record turntable, power operated windows and seat and deluxe heater-defroster. Loaded, but without passengers, the car weighed 4490 pounds of which 53½ per cent (2400 pounds) was on the front wheels and 46½ per cent (2090 pounds) was on the rear wheels. The weight distribution affected a very nice "balance" that was reflected in the roadability, which, for practical purposes was good in all respects, except that like other Chrysler Corp. products, the suspension, shock absorbers and anti-roll stabilizer bar were all on the "soft" side. This permitted a noticeable degree of "roll" on turns and "nosedive" during severe braking, but the "pitching" effect was non-existant due to the 120 inch wheelbase. Of course, the redeeming feature here was the excellent quality of the ride.

Handling ease, driver and passenger comfort and lack of fatigue factors were all in the Chrysler Corp. tradition, which is first-class. Visibility in all directions was excellent, even with the top up. All accessory switches and controls were within easy driver reach, but the markings were not too legible. The only major point of criticism is that the "coaxial" power steering is entirely too easy and consequently, lacks the necessary "feel-of-the-road" for completely worry-free driving. This requires some "getting used to" and, in a car the size of the DeSoto, power steering is practically an essential.

The Chrysler brakes were, as always, really excellent, even during some brutal punishment, and brake "fade" was never a factor to contend with. The drums are 12 inches in diameter front and back and the brakes contain a total effective lining area of 251 square inches, equivalent to 17.8 square inches per

4500 lb. DeSoto showed surprising agility in acceleration.

Racer indicates front of engine in relation to wheel center.

The roomy engine compartment assures very good accessibility.   *Good instrument, control layout in lavishly-appointed interior.*

New and bigger engine sparks DeSoto performance

Photos by Al Paloczy

pound of car weight. In addition to the lining area, the front brakes are of the time-proven two-leading shoe design. The stroke of the wide brake pedal was short, due to the vacuum power booster, but it possessed a good feel.

The pushbutton PowerFlite and drive train to the rear wheels is normal to other cars of the Chrysler line. When starting in drive, full throttle upshifts occur at about 55 mph and full throttle downshifts occur up to about 50 mph. The rear axle gear ratio of our test car was a favorable 3.73.

The best acceleration times were obtained in drive range with a normal upshift. The average zero to 60 mph time was 9.8 seconds, rather surprising for a 4500 pound car. The average zero to 80 mph time was an equally good 17.2 seconds. No doubt the 3.73's helped in this respect and, although we didn't have time to check it, the fuel/air mixture was obviously very close to right, as was the spark advance curve. From this it can be fairly accurately calculated that maximum road horsepower was in the vicinity of 140 or so.

In the matter of fuel economy, the DeSoto again showed characteristics of its Chrysler Corp. parentage. For the acceleration runs, we averaged 11.4 mpg; in the city, the average was 12.3 mpg; in the mountains the mileage was 13.7; on the highway at steady and legal speeds, a very creditable 17.0 mpg was recorded for an overall average of 13.6 mpg. As with other engines with a hemispherical combustion chamber, the DeSoto

exhibited a thirst for the best quality gasolines, otherwise detonation was likely to be encountered.

The DeSoto 330 cubic inch engine is rated at 255 brake horsepower at 4400 rpm and 350 pounds-feet of torque at 3200 rpm. The engines are strictly DeSoto and not left-over Chryslers. The bore is $3\frac{23}{32}$ inches and the stroke is $3\frac{51}{64}$ inches, which shows that DeSoto, for one, is gradually moving away from the "over-square" school, but whether they're "graduating" or being "demoted" to the longer-stroke class hasn't as yet been determined. The compression ratio is 8½ to 1. With the fully machined hemispherical chambers, double rocker arm shafts are used on each head. Intake valve diameter is 1.940 inches and exhaust valve diameter is 1¾ inches. The intake and exhaust ports are quite short and appear to be well streamlined and of generous cross-sectional area. The intake valve opens at 15 degrees before top center, closes 57 degrees after bottom center, duration 252 degrees, lift at valve .381 of an inch. Exhaust opens 49 degrees before bottom center, closes 15 degrees after top center, duration 244 degrees, lift at valve .357 of an inch. Carburetion is supplied by a single four-barrel Carter WCFB-2311-S, an excellent carburetor.

A person desiring more performance (and who doesn't these days?) has a pretty good built-in supply of some of the necessary pieces because of the interchangeability between standard DeSoto parts and those of the DeSoto (*Continued on page* **59**)

As Editor Parks hangs on, Racer applies the king-size binders. Brakes were excellent but considerable "nosedive" was evident.

DE SOTO

has a new economy job and some industry firsts.

Engines	Cylinders	Carburetor Barrels	Displacement	H.P.	Torque	Bore & Stroke	Comp. Ratio
Firesweep	8	2	325	245	320	3.69 x 3.80	8.5
Firesweep (optional)	8	4	325	260	335	3.69 x 3.80	8.5
Firedome	8	2	341	270	350	3.78 x 3.80	9.25
Fireflite	8	4	341	295	375	3.78 x 3.80	9.25

TO BROADEN its line, DeSoto has brought out a new venture for it, a price leader. It will be called the Firesweep, and will use a Dodge-sized chassis and engine with nearly four more inches of overall length and, supposedly, more prestige than on the lesser line. It comes with either a two- or four-barrel carburetor; the latter provides an additional boot of 15 horsepower, and both are content without Ethyl fuel. Interior dimensions are practically identical with those of the Dodges, or, for that matter, the Plymouths.

But when a rear seat is as low as they are getting this year, a little extra legroom can make a difference. The tape measure shows but a scant half-inch more space here than in the Dodge, yet we were more comfortable. The middle spot is now definitely for poor relations, even in the sedans. There just isn't room for springs.

The Firesweep is a rather restrained, even austere, car for this year of good living. From the driver's seat you look out over a more massive hood than that on the lower-priced lines, yet there is no impression of great size. As on bigger DeSotos, there's a broad, hooded, Lincoln-like panel. A red line moves across to indicate your speed (in steadier fashion than on the

Dodge) and the old familiar four gauges are blessedly present.

The car's behavior showed the family characteristics, and it's a far better car to drive, ride in, or stop in than ever before. Power steering, at least on this car, lacked desirable directional stability. Whipping the wheel to one side produced, instead of a quick return to straight ahead, a wild dart toward the guard rail of the track.

The two bigger DeSotos are both fancier and more powerful than their little sister. They, and all the more expensive cars in the line, will knock on a regular fuel diet. As has become customary, the Fireflite overlaps the Chrysler Windsor—now a low-cost version a little like DeSoto's own Firesweep—in power, and for '57 it equals the Chrysler Saratoga, which replaces last year's Windsor. Thoroughly mixed up now?

The three-seat Explorer wagons will introduce new Goodyear tires with independent air chambers, and hence no spare. They can carry the car at customary speeds for up to 100 miles after damage and should be an important contribution to safety on our ever more crowded roads. And think of never having to change a tire on a Sunday drive! The feminine vote should swing whole-heartedly to this innovation.

Turn your key (one way to close, the other to open) and the rear window scoots up or down.

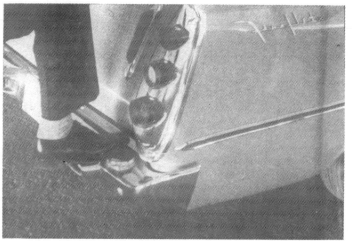

As though into an old rumble seat, you'll enter the wagon's rear-facing seat like this.

What's New?

New, smaller, lower-priced DeSoto called Firesweep . . . Torsion-bar front suspension . . . Wrap-over-top windshield on convertibles; wrap-over-top back window on Fireflite hardtop . . . Dramatic new station wagon with third seat facing to rear . . . Glamorous styling, even when compared to other '57 Chrysler products.

Your Choice

With the 122-inch wheelbase Firesweep, DeSoto plunges into a price class that within the Chrysler family has been occupied only by Dodge. The odd part about the whole maneuver is that Firesweeps are built for DeSoto by Dodge. This baby DeSoto offers many advantages besides price. All interior dimensions except two are equal to the "larger" Firedomes and Fireflites. Slight differences in front and rear legroom cancel one another.

All three series offer two- and four-door hardtops and four-door sedans. Convertibles are restricted to the larger 126-inch wheelbase chassis; four-door station wagons with or without the rear-facing third seat are available on both wheelbases.

At one time, it was planned to move the spare tire on these three-seat models into a spot beneath the right rear fender, with access gained through a removable panel in the lower part of the fender as in Plymouth and Dodges. Fortunately, Goodyear came up with their Captive-Air nylon tire, so this expensive alternative became as unnecessary as the spare tire itself. This trouble-proof tire is standard on the wagon. No one, however, has devised a substitute for the gas tank, which had to be moved under the left rear fender.

DeSoto's newly wide range of models, bracketing 93 per cent of cars sold outside the lowest price range, can be taken as another indication that Chrysler Corp.

plans soon to set up separate dealerships for each of its makes. Now, if DeSoto dealers lose the Plymouth, they can still tackle Buick, Oldsmobile, and Mercury competition and be as versatile as at least the latter two.

DeSoto Power

The Firesweep engine, in either 245 or 260 horsepower form (the difference lies in two- and four-barrel carburetors), is basically Dodge. This single-rocker-arm design uses "polyspherical" (better called hemispheroid) combustion chambers, and spark plugs are easily accessible.

The well-proved Firedome and Fireflite V8s have received the usual boost in displacement, compression ratio, and degree of cam lift. They check out at 270 and 295 horsepower, respectively. The potential of this smooth-running, double-rocker-arm, hemispherical combustion chamber design seems limitless. It was first introduced in 1952 and puts out more and more almost effortlessly.

Firesweeps offer a choice of two push-button automatics, the three-speed Torque-flite and two-speed Powerflite, as well as three-speed manual and overdrive. Fireflites are all equipped with the Torque-flite; Firedomes make it an option over the little-sold manual box.

DeSoto on the Road

Front-end torsion bars, called "Torsion-Aire," do wonders for DeSoto ride and handling. During the press preview in Detroit, it was demonstrated by driving a car at speed over simulated railroad ties. This was on a large stage, and any loss of directional control, front or rear, could easily have resulted in injury to chorus girls, standing within inches of the car's path. The DeSoto (as well as all other Chrysler products) swept over this truly

rough surface with level body and complete freedom from skittishness.

Incorporated into the system is ball-joint mounting of the front wheels, giving greater stability while cornering and greatly reduced freedom from dive while braking. A manual adjustment built into the rear mount of each torsion bar permits correction for front-end sag should this condition occur after many miles of use. The full range of DeSoto power boosts is available on any model, and quick-stopping Center-Plane brakes are standard.

Inside Your DeSoto

DeSoto, always noted for one of the best-looking if not most readable instrument panels, does not lose its status by switching to a high-mounted, thermometer-type speed indicator centered over the lesser gauges. "Black light" at night prevents annoying reflections, and the driver really appreciates the flood of illumination thrown out ahead by the optional dual headlight installation. Unfortunately, this is available in larger DeSotos only.

Interiors, throughout the range, seem to offer a little more for the money, and quality of workmanship is excellent. This is one of the hidden benefits of relatively low production. Those with small children will appreciate the left-of-driver location of the transmission control, and the children of parents who own one of the new wagons should be fascinated by the prospect of seeing the world go by in reverse as they cruise down the highway.

Why Buy?

Styling that stands out, even among its advanced brothers . . . Adequate power unobtrusively served up . . . Big car luxury in a reasonably sized package . . . Constantly improving depreciation rate

THE EXPLORER wagons, like this DeSoto Fireflite, feature a rearward-facing third seat, power rear window, and special flat-proof tires.

GREATER WRAP-AROUND

5 INCHES LOWER

BIGGER FINS

RECESSED HANDLES

V GRILLE

14-INCH WHEELS

BALL JOINTS and torsion bars combine to make the '57 DeSoto a much better handling car with an excellent ride.

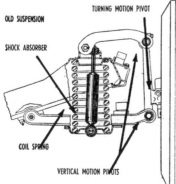

OLD SUSPENSION

TURNING MOTION PIVOT

SHOCK ABSORBER

COIL SPRING

VERTICAL MOTION PIVOTS

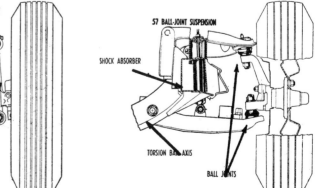

57 BALL-JOINT SUSPENSION

SHOCK ABSORBER

TORSION BAR AXIS

BALL JOINTS

DE SOTO

By JAMES WHIPPLE

IN ADDITION to the revolutionary changes of the '57 models that are Chrysler Corporation's styling and engineering changes (Flight-Sweep styling, Torsion-Aire ride) De Soto has invaded the lower-medium price field (Dodge, Studebaker, Mercury and Pontiac) with its new Firesweep models.

Firesweep De Sotos are an interesting hybrid of Dodge chassis and De Soto body parts. The Firesweep's powerplant is the 325-cubic-inch V-8 used on Dodges as Red Ram (245 bhp two barrel carburetor) and Super Red Ram (four barrel carburetor and 260 bhp.) Either engine is available and both will operate on today's "regular" grades of fuel.

The chassis of Firesweep models is the same 122-inch wheelbase unit used by Dodge. However, bumper and rear end overhang of the De Soto gives a length of 215.8 inches compared to Dodge's 212-inch overall length and the longer Firedome and Fireflite models overall, of 218 inches. Wheelbases of the latter models (they'll probably get called the "big" De Sotos), are 126 inches, as are the three Chrysler lines.

In actual fact the Firesweep consists of a De Soto grille topped off by Dodge front fender panels, hood and cowl, followed by the De Soto body shell which has one-half inch more rear seat leg room than the Dodge. The trunk and rear fenders are, of course, De Soto.

Unfortunately we have not been able to test a Firesweep De Soto at this time, so we're unable to report directly on the "under-the-paint" merger of Chrysler Corporation's lower-medium and medium-priced divisions.

What we do know is that the '57 Fireflite and Firedome De Sotos offer a pretty hard-to-beat package of high-performance transportation.

After testing the Dodge, the first difference we noted was the even greater quietness of the car, both at speed on the highway and in traffic Not that the Dodge ever came near to being objectionably noisy — we were just less conscious of speed noises, wind, tire roar, fan, engine and transmission hum. De Soto is a car in which you can cruise comfortably at 80 mph if road surface, traffic conditions and the law permit.

At such speeds on turnpikes or super highways the De Soto is very steady, yet has none of the harsh, vibrating ride characteristics of the tautly suspended roadable cars of the past. The reason is, of course, the senior version of the "Chrysler family's" torsion-bar suspended chassis and the new lower center of gravity.

We began to realize what the De Soto's superior roadability meant on a long trip over a cross country

Price range (Factory list price)
$2,479 (Firesweep four-door sedan)
to $3,498 (Fireflite convertible coupe).

DE SOTO
is the car
for you

if... You like a big roomy car that's as easy to handle as one of the low-priced cars.

if... You are looking for an unparalleled combination of riding comfort and roadability.

if... You appreciate really new and different styling that is the result of functional improvements and not just change for the sake of change.

if... You want the most efficient engine design and advanced chassis engineering in the De Soto price field.

DE SOTO SPECIFICATIONS

ENGINES	FIRESWEEP V8	FIREDOME V8	FIREFLITE V8
Bore and stroke	3.69 in. x 3.80 in.	3.78 in. x 3.80 in.	3.78 in. x 3.80 in.
Displacement	325 cu. in.	341 cu. in.	341 cu. in.
Compression ratio	8.5:1	9.25:1	9.25:1
Max. brake horsepower	245 @ 4400 rpm	270 @ 4600 rpm	295 @ 4600 rpm
Max. torque	320 @ 2400 rpm	350 @ 2400 rpm	375 @ 2800 rpm

DIMENSIONS	FIRESWEEP	FIREDOME, FIREFLITE	
Wheelbase	122 in.	126 in.	
Overall length	215.8 in.	218 in.	
Overall width	78.2 in.	78.2 in.	
Overall height	57 in.	57 in.	

TRANSMISSIONS	Standard synchromesh, PowerFlite, TorqueFlite.

De Soto Firesweep is new entry into lower-medium price field. Firesweep is hybrid, has Dodge chassis, De Soto body shell. Car combines Dodge front fender panels, hood, cowl, with De Soto grille. Headlamps are mounted under Dodge-like overhanging "brows."

expressway where we maintained a steady and relaxed pace of 65 miles per hour. Other cars (of all makes) would pass us at 70 or even 75 on straightaways, but on the long, sweeping curves we found that we had to ease off, much to our surprise, to keep the big De Soto from climbing into their trunks.

The softness of ride combined with stability has to be experienced to be appreciated. We have experienced stable roadable chassis in driving a good many genuine sports cars of competition calibre, and we have felt the ultimate in marshmallow-smooth riding qualities (last year's De Sotos and Chryslers), but never a combination such as found on the '57 Chrysler line. We are not trying to say that the '57 De Soto has the roadholding ability of a Porsche sportscar, in which design accommodation for only two passengers has been provided, and in which baggage must be severely limited.

What we are saying is that the Porsche owner will feel far more at ease in a '57 De Soto, (or Plymouth or Dodge, etc.) than he will in any other American production car.

Comparison of De Soto and other Chrysler products with sports cars

stops short at the steering wheel. Chrysler steering is designed for the super-market parking lot rather than the race course, and quite rightly so. To provide the very necessary ease of handling needed by those who must drive in congested traffic conditions, (and who doesn't these days?) there is either power steering or very high ratio manual steering (ie., many revolutions of steering wheel to swing front wheels from lock to lock). This means that it's fairly easy to handle the car in traffic and park it, but difficult to maneuver the car quickly at high speeds simply because there isn't time to crank your steering wheel while taking a sharp corner at speed. Power steering remedies this, but when it is installed on a De Soto, (or other Chrysler products), you must learn to steer "by the seat of your pants" because all resistance to turning which gives the driver an idea of how sharply he can turn the wheel at a given speed on a given surface vanishes with the application of "full time" power steering. And, unfortunately, so does conventional caster action (tendency of wheels to return to the straight ahead position during and after turning).

The De Soto that we tested was Fireflite with the "big" 295 bhp engine coupled to Torque-Flite automatic transmission. Performance with this power team was up to hot rod standards. It is almost impossible to operate the De Soto with the accelerator floored without exceeding every speed limit in the U. S. On long hills of eight per cent gradient the car rolls up to 70 mph with the throttle short of the cut-in point of the second pair of venturi in the four-barrel carbureter. When you floor the accelerator the De Soto leaps to 85 mph.

When you add this flashing acceleration to effortless steering (power assisted), easy, well-controlled braking and the De Soto's highly roadable chassis, you have a car that is big but handles like a small, lightweight car. Only when you're trying to maneuver the car into a snug berth in a crowded parking lot do you become aware of the car's 18-foot length and 6½-foot width.

One of the many things we liked about the De Soto was the excellent vision for both driver and passengers. The wide sweep of windshield brings the overhead traffic lights back into vision again, to say nothing of highly placed street signs. De Soto's back-

Signal tower tail lights are distinctive De Soto feature, Heightened fins hold separate brake lights, turn indicators. Chrome covered exhaust extensions rest underneath tail light assembly.

ward-slanted corner posts on the deeply wrapped windshield are *the* efficient design for wraparounds. The pillar is back out of the normal arc of vision at eye-level while at the same time slanted forward so that the corner of the windshield doesn't form an awkward "dogleg" that juts into the front door opening at knee-level. Other benefits in vision brought about by the greatly lowered chassis and body are the location of the rear view mirror at the bottom of the windshield out of the line of vision instead of suspended from the upper rim smack in the middle of the windshield. This seems like a trivial detail (it's on all Chrsler products), but the reduction in eye-strain must be experienced.

SUMMING UP: De Soto is a car that has just about everything, and if enough people can be persuaded to try it on for size it could move toward the top sales spot in its price class. Room, luggage space, ease of control, luxury, styling, performance, riding comfort, roadability, durable construction are all tops on the De Soto. It's equally well suited to trips across town or across the continent. ●

DE SOTO CHECK LIST

5 CHECKS MEANS TOP RATING

Category	Description	Rating
PERFORMANCE	Outstanding with 295 bhp V-8 and Torque-Flite transmission. More than adequate on the 270 bhp Firedome and 245 bhp Firesweep models.	✔✔ ✔ / ✔✔
STYLING	Without the contrasting color spear located near the bottom of the body, De Soto has one of the simplest and most striking lines of any of the '57s.	✔✔ ☐ / ✔✔
RIDING COMFORT	This is De Soto's highest card. It is without doubt the most comfortable-riding car in its price class. And in this consideration we include all factors that make for comfort: quiet operation, absence of wind noise, upholstery and seating positions as well as stability of the chassis.	✔✔ ✔ / ✔✔
INTERIOR DESIGN	Tops for accessibility to seats in four-door sedans, and for all all around vision and legroom. Seating position may be a bit low and demand farther outstretching of legs than people are used to, but it all adds up to a very high level of comfort.	✔✔ ☐ / ✔✔
ROADABILITY	De Soto's roadability was good last year, has moved ahead of others in its class this year. The car is stable and free from sway on all types of roads.	✔✔ ✔ / ✔✔
EASE OF CONTROL	Excellent with power steering, although some drivers may feel that De Soto's full-time power steering doesn't offer sufficient road sense. Torque-Flite transmission offers good engine braking control on downgrades.	✔✔ ☐ / ✔✔
ECONOMY	Not a prime consideration in a large powerful car like De Soto, but if driven at average highway speeds the 295-bhp Fireflite will give close to 15 miles per gallon.	✔✔ ☐ / ✔☐
SERVICEABILITY	Except for spark plugs deeply buried in valve mechanism, De Soto engine and chassis components are easier to service than other cars in its class.	✔✔ ☐ / ✔✔
WORKMANSHIP	Above average in its price class. Paint job and exterior trim was excellent. Upholstery very good but some evidence of improperly fitted interior trim.	✔✔ / ✔✔
VALUE PER DOLLAR	We feel that De Soto offers more luxury transportation value than other cars in its price class. This must be balanced against a somewhat higher rate of depreciation.	✔✔ ☐ / ✔✔

DE SOTO OVERALL RATING ... 4.2 CHECKS

THE DESOTO CONVERTIBLE, A MODEL TYPE RARELY ROAD TESTED, PROVED TO BE SURPRISINGLY GOOD IN THE ACCELERATION CHECKS.

WRAP-OVER WINDSHIELD, available only on the convertible, does not have excessive distortion. However, angle of the glass catches more dirt, makes frequent cleaning necessary.

DE SOTO ROAD TEST

LIKE all the other Chrysler Corporation makes of cars, DeSoto is all-new for 1957. About all that has been retained from the '56 model is the engine. The body and virtually all other major units inside or under it have been completely changed, some of them rather drastically.

The total result, therefore, is pretty different from what has gone before it. Yet the combination is not quite so surprising, as say in the case of Plymouth, since DeSoto seems to have been heading in this general direction right along.

In brief, what in the early 1950s was a fairly fuddy-duddy automobile has blossomed into something as sprightly and as stylish as they come these days. The transition that began in 1955 is at its end—from here on they only can polish of this gem of the middle-priced class.

The foregoing indicates that the DeSoto test car was an especially interesting one. It was. Further, the body type was (1) a convertible, a body type infrequently encountered in testing; (2) the car was equipped with true dual headlights, the first available for extensive city and highway night driving; (3) the windshield was the compound-curve type (which wraps over as well as around), another first in testing.

In addition to all this, it was discovered that the DeSoto ranks as a far better-than-average accelerator.

The takeoff from a standing start was most commendable in view of the fact that the engine involved was the middle-sized DeSoto offering for 1957—the 341-cubic-inch version with a two-barrel carburetor rated at 270 hp. Another standard engine, with 20 more horses via a four-barrel carburetor, naturally would be more potent. And DeSoto also builds the 1957 edition of the Adventurer, rated at 345 hp, which on the basis of what was uncovered in this test, should be numbered among the hottest cars of the year.

The test car was a Firedome convertible fresh from TV

STEERING POSITION is absolutely unsurpassed. Dash layout is excellent, except for hard-to-read thermometer-type speedo and rearview mirror that's subject to vibrations. The top is padded.

stunt films, involving apparently rugged use since some body damage was in partial repair. Padding for movie camera mounts still were present. In general, however, the car was in excellent condition, gave out with only one rattle when the windows and top were down.

Power assist items were steering, brakes and seat. The heater featured simple controls and operated most efficiently. The radio produced adequate but unspectacular reception.

Overall styling of the DeSoto is excellent and it contributes to Chrysler Corporation's current leadership in this area of design. If it has any weak point worth mentioning, it probably is in the grille, a clean layout by domestic standards but one which probably will not win universal approval by a long shot. The test convertible, just 55 inches from top to ground, hits a new high in lowness. Nonetheless, entrance and exit are easy, seating and visibility are superb.

The dash, like the rest of the corporation's, spurns flashing lights and sticks to simple and readable dials arranged in functional round casings. Only the horizontal thermometer-style speedometer keeps the instrument cluster from getting a 100 per cent rating.

In DeSoto's lineup, the compound-curve or wrap-over windshield is available only in convertibles. Its glass area is positively enormous, contributes immensely to vision and a feeling of contact with the road. Distortion is little for all practical purposes. The makers claim some benefits in reduced drafts when the top is lowered; this windshield does do, but it by no means eliminates the breezes completely. They are heading in the right direction but this is only one step—not the entire answer.

One disadvantage with the windshield, one which had not been anticipated, was the tendency to dirty quickly. Apparently the slope or angle of the glass does not permit dust to slide off as easily as on the conventional type. Stops for cleaning are more frequent.

Night driving with the new dual headlights did not provide any obvious benefits over an up-to-date single lamp system. Perhaps measurements with precision instruments would establish some degree of improvement, but these are not readily appreciated by the unscientific eye of the driver. It has been suspected that the duals are a styling device, rather than a major advance in illumination.

In performance, with a 0-60 mph time of 9.7 seconds, the DeSoto straddles the line between the average and hot cars by 1957 standards. This, it is emphasized again, with only a two-barrel carburetor. Floorboarding the throttle results in an excessive amount of wheelspin, but once the tires take hold the car really moves.

The transmission is a big improvement over the two-speed automatic box of '56; introduced last year in the Imperial it's now spread out over all the corporation's makes. Only change in the pushbuttons is an extra button for punching, which in normal driving is entirely superfluous.

The DeSoto's strongest point is one that can't be shown in photos or expressed in figures. It is a quality that was discovered in earlier tests of the Plymouth and the Dodge.

A car, in the final analysis, is something you ride in or drive. In the case of the DeSoto, its steering ease and general roadability are absolutely unsurpassed. It has to be experienced to be appreciated. Body roll is at a minimum, corners are as flat as can be, and driver and passengers find something honestly new in American car comfort. This is coupled with the finest seating position and steering wheel location ever created in Detroit. With the large windshield, low-slung cowl and broad, flat hood, the driver feels closer to the road.

If there is a catch in all this, it only is that the DeSoto is a big, heavy machine and cannot be powered around a sharp turn without a measure of caution. The secure feeling, enhanced by the power steering, is so great that it's deceptive.

The quality of the DeSoto, in terms of materials and workmanship, is up from preceding models. It's good, better than before, but could be improved further. One chronic weak spot (common on the corporation's cars for several years) are the door and trunk locks.

What does this all add up to? If you're big-car minded, like the prestige, size, etc., of something more than the low-priced class, the DeSoto is quite a package. And as a bonus, you may also keep in mind that for less money you also get one of the top three luxury bodies. ●

DESOTO TEST DATA

Test Car: 1957 DeSoto Firedome convertible
Basic Price: $3305
Engine: 341-cubic-inch ohv V-8
Compression Ratio: 9.25-to-1
Horsepower: 270 @ 4600 rpm
Torque: 350 @ 2400 rpm
Dimensions: Length 218 inches, width 78, height 55, tread 61 front 60 rear, wheelbase 126
Dry Weight: 4100 lbs.
Transmission: Three-speed Torque-Flite torque converter
Acceleration: 0-30 mph 3.4 seconds, 0-45 mph 6, 0-60 mph 9.7 seconds
Gas Mileage: 14.5 mpg average
Speedometer Corrections: Indicated 30, 45 and 60 mph are actual 28, 42 and 55 mph, respectively

ENTRANCE AND EXIT are easy, despite fact that overall height is as low as they come. The reason, common to all 1957 Chrysler Corporation makes, is that the forward post and windshield do not jut as far into door area. DeSoto provides a place for the license plate by recessing a mount into the trunk lid. Rear window must be unzipped before the top is lowered, but takes less than a minute.

The Adventures of DE SOTO

Story and Photos by William Carroll

SUSPENSION, BRAKES, handling were given work-out during "Stop and Go Tests" at first session of Daytona Speedweeks.

S NEAK TREAT OF '58 is DeSoto's Adventurer series, a gutty hardtop and convertible duo for the fellow who wants something different. We ran a hardtop, which like an old shoe, made us feel at home from the very first mile.

Before picking up the car in Detroit, we spent a lot of time talking with George Gale, assistant chief engineer for DeSoto, who said, "Our approach to designing the Adventurer was to have a car with an appeal of its own. Not a competition car — but performance-proved transportation that would be pleasant to drive every day of the year."

Mr. Gale also told us that to achieve this package they used the top series (Fireflite) and made extensive comparison tests between standard suspension and competition lashing before deciding to leave the stock DeSoto ride alone. They use the same basic Chrysler "B" engine shared with some other models of Dodge and Plymouth and installed a hot Chrysler-designed cam, dual-breaker-point distributor, cooler spark plugs and a most unique DeSoto dual carburetor intake manifold. The manifold was selected only after lengthy laboratory tests that showed the "B" engine to be more responsive to dual four-throat carburetion than other usual combinations. By careful selection of production cylin-

der heads the Adventurer runs a 10.25 to 1 ratio, with heavier valve springs to keep hydraulic actuated valves under control. Other changes over regular production include ¼-inch larger exhaust piping, tuned mufflers and optional rear axle ratios from 2.92 to 3.91 to 1. For the "it's gotta feel like a sports car" driver, "export" shock absorbers and springs are available at extra cost.

Speaking of cost brings up an interesting point. DeSoto's Adventurer is exactly the same size (except for length of fins) as a Chrysler 300-D, weighs 340 pounds less, has 35 fewer horses and is almost $1000 cheaper. This is what we meant by a "sneak treat." Though only 1500 hardtops and 350 convertibles are scheduled for 1958, the price is mighty low for such a custom package.

NEW FOR '58 are such bits as four tubular struts extending from the fenders to the cowl to reduce fender weave found in so many cars, a special sealing and coating technique in body construction that seals the body so well our heater blower couldn't force air into the car unless a window was opened slightly, a tremendous bubble canopy windshield that allows you to see overhead traffic lights, plus two-inch

ADVENTURER with car tester Bill Carroll at the Detroit factory.

DE SOTO on hard-packed Florida Beach prior to test.

AFTER DRAGGIN' for 200 yards down straightaway, we had to try to stop with front wheels on a line one-foot wide.

longer rear springs for a softer ride. The rear axle is mounted forward of the spring center to a forward section of the rear spring that is seven times stiffer than the rear section.

The new "B" engine has many new approaches to engine design when compared to a '57 installation. Bearing areas have been increased 25 per cent, crankshaft overlap area is doubled, compression ratio and cubic inches are raised, and lightweight stamped rocker arms are used. Best of all, the "B" engine is 60 pounds lighter than last year's V8.

After George filled us in on engineering behind the Adventurer we headed for the factory parking lot. Buried in a field of nearly snowbound cars was a hardtop which much to our surprise started promptly and kept on running in the 20° weather. A quick fill with gas and we headed over icy roads to Daytona, Florida, and more cold weather.

This was a strange trip. Most high-performance cars have such strong personalities the first thousand miles are spent getting used to them. Not so the DeSoto. It had no bad habits, behaved well on ice and slushy roads, went around corners with all the confidence of a well sprung torsion bar setup and rode softly enough to please the most tender tail. Credit should be given the Adventurer's long (126-inch)

wheelbase and widest tread of any car in its price class.

During these first three days we couldn't help but compare DeSoto with a 300-D driven cross-country (Jan. MOTOR TREND). Space the same. Feel the same. DeSoto more softly sprung on 1.04-inch torsion bars (300-D uses 1.11-inch bars) and passenger car shocks. Interior of the DeSoto a suave gold on gold fabric mixed with vinyl trim; the 300-D uses top-grain beige leather. One set of instruments was as handy as the other; DeSoto uses a horizontal red-line speedometer; a pointer on circular disc for the 300-D.

But there are differences in the cars, both on the negative and positive side. An Adventurer rides better than a 300-D. But it shakes more (300-D's frame 474 pounds versus Adventurer's 318 pounds) and is noisier. The 300-D handles better over 80 mph, the Adventurer better at lower speeds. The "B" engine is lighter and easier to service than the 300-D. But the 300-D engine turns 326 fewer revolutions per mile, has a longer stroke and seems to have more "umph" in the upper end. Then there is a $1000 difference in price, favoring the Adventurer. Luckily we had a chance to put it through its paces at Daytona, making comparisons with some mighty potent machinery.

DE SOTO

FIRST THING WE TRIED was the "Stop and Go Test" set up by NASCAR (see "Public Proving Ground," MT, Apr. '58) to test suspension, brakes and handling. And that it did. Over-eager drivers ran out of brakes, clutches or power steering belts as Detroit's best were driven like they had never been driven before. At the starter's send-off we'd drag madly up one 200-yard straightaway and try to stop with front wheels on a line one-foot wide. Shift to low and turn right into a 25-foot-deep parking area. Stop. Hit reverse and back out of the parking area across the simulated intersection into another 25-foot parking area. Stop without knocking over any of the boundary markers. Punch the DRIVE button and turn left up another 200-yard straight to stop, start, park, back up and go again. Twenty intersections. Optimum time: 6 minutes 20 seconds. And points off your score for missing the white line, running off course or knocking down markers.

How did the DeSoto and Carroll do? Not too well. Our score was a shameful 351 points in 7 minutes 58.8 seconds. We *did* treat the spectators to a most spectacular spin-out on dry pavement when our foot dove too deeply into horse-power as we pulled from an intersection. This demonstration knocked 25 points off our final score.

Fun on the beach began after "Stop and Go Tests" were completed. It was so cold that roadster owners were buying hot dogs just to hold in their hands and bring life to cold-numbed fingers. In spite of such natural obstacles to comfort we were able to have the Adventurer timed in the Flying Mile and for acceleration potential.

While waiting in line we pulled hubcaps from the Adven-turer and filled tires to 50 pounds for maximum safety at speed. As the tide went out an old pickup truck ambled down the course setting rubber guide cones every hundred yards. On a return trip markers were set on the other side to complete outlining the five mile beach straightaway course (two miles to gain speed, a mile in the trap and two miles to slow down). Though called a straightaway, it's not really very straight. The beach curves slightly, and during the entire run cars are always turning slightly to follow the curve, which on slippery sand calls for light fingers on the wheel.

On the north run we hit 116.656 mph, then did 123.035 on our south run for an average of 119.760. Though beaten by 10 Pontiacs and two 300-Ds, in the case of the Pontiacs they were cars with engines specifically designed and tuned by racing mechanics to really fly, while the 300-Ds cost $1000 more, have more horsepower and upper-end perform-ance. All in all the Adventurer's showing was impressive for a "straight from the factory" production car not specifically tuned for top speed, running power steering, automatic trans-mission and loaded with weighty, power-sapping comfort devices.

NASCAR scheduled Wednesday, February 19th, for ac-celeration timing with class breakdowns identical to those used for the Flying Mile tests. Of 22 cars entered we came near the middle at 81.154 mph. Daytona acceleration runs are unlike timing at a dragstrip, as not only do cars start on a sand beach (in which many a leadfoot has buried his chances for winning time) but they run a measured mile from the "Start" line to the end of the trap. Results are an-nounced in *average* miles per hour over the mile, based on the length of time it takes to enter the measured mile from a standing start and leave it at top speed.

With two weeks of fun over, we replaced the DeSoto hub-caps, had salt spray washed off the body and headed for home by way of New Orleans, Houston and Yuma. We ran the uneventful first day from Daytona to New Orleans (651.1 miles) in a little over 11 hours, averaging 58.13 mph and 12.75 miles per gallon of Mobilgas. The following day we slowed to visit a number of auto dealers, traveled 398.8 miles, averaged 14.66 mpg at 46.92 miles an hour.

The third day found our Adventurer battering its way through one of Texas' worst windstorms with 75-mile-an-hour breezes tearing tops off buildings while searching for people. Although we were able to average 67.55 mph for the 675.5-mile run, gas mileage fell off to 10.81 mpg as a result of the head-winds. On the fourth day we ran out of

continued on page 59

COMPARISON CHART

	DeSoto Golden Adventurer Hardtop	Chrysler 300-D Hardtop
Price	$4016	$5108
Wheelbase	126 inches	126 inches
Horsepower	345 @ 5000 rpm	380 @ 5200 rpm
Weight	3965 lbs.	4305 lbs.
Hp to Weight	11.4 hp per lb.	11.3 hp per lb.
Compression Ratio	10.25 to 1	10 to 1
Tire Size	8.50 x 14	9.00 x 14
Cross-Country gas consumption average	12.6 mpg	13.6 mpg
Standing-start one-mile acceleration run	81.154 mph	87.485 mph
Flying mile	119.760 mph	126.000 mph

De Soto Adventurer

continued from page 58

Texas roads (though it seemed to take forever), crossed New Mexico and spent the night in Yuma, Ariz. Total distance 692.3 miles, driving time 10.1 hours, average mph 68.54, average mpg 12.57. A few hours of driving the next day brought us into Los Angeles where totaling trip records showed the car had scooted 2706.2 miles from Florida to California at an average road speed of 60.95 mph and averaged 12.4 miles per gallon of Mobilgas.

Cost of speed is indicated by comparing the different days' runs. At 46.92 mph we averaged 14.66 mpg. At 58.13 mph, 12.75 mpg. At 68.54 mph, 12.57 mpg. Compare this with 13.59 mpg during a similar cross-country run in a 300-D at an average speed of 58.9 miles an hour. Point! The 300-D was running a 2.93 to 1 rear axle, unwinding the engine 2147 revolutions per mile. The DeSoto uses a 3.31 to 1 ratio which lets the engine turn 2473 revolutions each mile. On this basis, the variation in rear axle ratio alone will save 300-D owners six gallons of gas every thousand miles, which at 35¢ a gallon figures to $2.10 per thousand. Plus reducing engine wear. *(Ed. Note: DeSoto has an optional 2.92 ratio available to order on new cars.)*

On the trip home a service station attendant remarked, "You writer guys have it made. All you do is say something nice about every car and the story's written." We told him, as you already know, nothing could be further from the truth. Then we showed him a number of things we questioned on the DeSoto. A dip-stick you almost can't get back in the tube, no head space for a tall person, seats too close to the floor, brakes that get hot and stay that way, higher noise level than luxury cars should have, and that doggone water leak over the forward part of the front door trim panel. Almost every Chrysler-built car since 1957 has this leak. And every dealer has the means to fix it. But new cars seem to leak just the same. Our particular car had some distortion in the windshield, and because it was in my line of vision, the factory is planning to put in new glass. As you know, most all cars have some distortion in the corners of the front glass, but no factory we have talked to wants you piloting a car with defective glass in front of the driver.

What I liked about the Adventurer is harder to pinpoint. Even after 4600 miles the hardtop is a real pleasant car. No bad habits, a good ride, plenty of performance, handling and braking with the best, decorator-designed interiors that pleased everyone at first sight, and a price structure that leaves little to quibble about. It's an impressive package. /MT

continued from page 46

"Adventurer." For example, the "Adventurer" double four-barrel manifold ("double log" type) and carburetors, camshaft, mechanical valve lifters, valve springs, pushrods, adjustable rocker arms and dual point ignition will fit standard DeSotos. Special parts such as "wilder" camshafts, scavenge type exhaust headers, high compression pistons, stroked crankshafts, battery and magneto ignitions, etc., are available for this engine as are special services for porting, valve gear work and precision balancing. There isn't much lacking in this line except a well-designed, balanced and heated three-carburetor manifold. A maximum rebore of $\frac{1}{8}$ of an inch to $3^{27}\!/\!_{32}$ inches is a practical proposition, as well as a $\frac{1}{4}$ of an inch stroke increase. The resulting 371 cubic inches should be enough for almost any job.

For those desiring moderate performance improvements, a compression ratio of 9.1 to 1 may be obtained by milling the heads .040 of an inch. From a compression ratio standpoint, this is about all the engine can stand with the best of present gasolines. The stock spark advance curve is pretty close, although the initial lead may be increased about four crankshaft degrees. Correcting the fuel/air ratio, a good sharp valve job and the alignment and matching of intake and exhaust ports should not be overlooked as details contributing to better all around performance.

The DeSoto engine needs no introduction to the competition world; rather, it's a part of that world and has been since the first V8 in 1952. In the subsequent five years, the DeSoto has proven its worth in countless competition applications such as boats, track and straightaway machines, sports cars and the ever-popular engine swap in passenger cars. The DeSotos are good engines and have been improving steadily each year. The only drawback is one of engine weight. The '56 V8 model checks out at about 780 pounds.

For chassis improvements to standard '56 DeSoto passenger cars, one should look again to the "Adventurer" series. These cars contain the options necessary to make the standard cars much more roadworthy, such as higher rate front coil and rear semi-elliptic springs and an anti-roll front stabilizer, as well as stiffer shock absorbers. These items would permit taking advantage of the inherently good balance and favorable weight distribution.

In all, the DeSoto is quite a satisfactory car if you like 'em big and roomy with excellent driver and passenger comfort and riding qualities. Yet, when you squeeze on the floorboard, you know things are happening under the hood. Some lucky guy is going to win some good transportation. Hm-m-m. Where are those Indy entry blanks?

A healthy member of the DeSoto family, the Firesweep is tested for its facts and faults

TESTING of a Chrysler product these days results in at least one universal appraisal: good handling. The De Soto preserves the family reputation and even maintains a slight advantage over the Plymouth and Dodge in the department of handling versus ride. This can be traced to the use of a front stabilizer bar which brings softer ride and still adequate handling in turns.

The car used for road testing was the Firesweep Sportsman two-door hardtop. It is the most inexpensive entry in the De Soto stable which is comprised of the Firesweep, Firedome, Fireflite and the limited Adventurer series.

The Firesweep's 280-hp, 350-cubic-inch displacement engine is very similar to that of the Plymouth Fury. Displacement and compression ratio are identical. The essential difference is found in the carburetion and valve timing. The De Soto carries only a single two-barrel carburetor.

These two barrels provide good initial acceleration but, at a point where the Fury begins to show outstanding performance, the Firesweep seems to fade out completely. On acceleration tests the best times were obtained by shifting the TorqueFlite transmission out of low at approximately 45 mph. Any attempt to wind the engine up to 55 or 60 mph accomplished nothing in the way of improving acceleration.

Another objection found for the Firesweep's carburetion system was its extreme turn sensitiveness. A cold engine combined with a sharp turn results in spilt fuel. The test car reeked of gasoline for fully two miles after taking such turns.

Carburetion and engine options are available in the De Soto line. The more expensive series boast a 361-cubic-inch displacement engine with longer duration cam and horsepower at 295 and 305 in the Firedome and Fireflite respectively. Four-barrel carburetion is offered and fuel injection of the Bendix breed can be obtained. Besides the tested TorqueFlite transmission PowerFlite is available.

On the inside of the De Soto the instrument panel presents a rather novel and unconventional appearance. Projecting above the level of the panel itself is a hood which contains the barograph-type speedometer. This is an easily viewed instrument which requires a minimum eye shift from road to reading. It is canted in such a way that the side to the driver's left sits an inch and a quarter closer to him than that on his right. Such beveling should cut down on back reflections but it also makes the instrument more readily checked by the good wife sitting in the righthand seat.

Directly below the speedometer are the locations of the light switch, the windshield wiper control knob, the ventilation and heater blower control and the

DE SOTO ROAD TEST

THE DE SOTO FIRESWEEP CALLS ON ALL 280 HORSES TO MAKE THE 32 PER CENT GRADE OF LOS ANGELES' FARGO HILL.

ignition switch. This is not a happy arrangement for operation of the switches while driving results in awkward movement in and around the wheel. More practical planning might see these controls moved down a step to the present location of the engine instruments and fuel gage in a row of four.

Minor irritation is caused by the glove compartment latching system. Pushing the button releases the catch but does not spring the door. Two hands must be used—one to pry and one to push.

The windshield and the rear window are both of the bubble variety which not only wraps-around but hovers-over. The added curves from deck and hood to the roof line are not at critical spots but they come up with an occasional view which is as distorted as the long look through a pop bottle.

The door handles are of the pull-out type used on some of the other Chrysler productions. Closed they are flush with the outer surface of the door. Opening merely requires placing the fingers under the bar and pulling. The normal outward motion required to extend the handle also opens the door. These are by

far the handiest handles in use today.

The rear bumper appears to have exhaust outlets incorporated into each end. These are only decoration for the true exhaust pipes project under the back of the body and are not visible from the exterior. The ends of these real exhausts are curved so that the gases are deflected downward.

The front bumper is quite massive but not all decoration. The top portion, which serves as the border of the radiator grille, has sturdy brackets attaching it directly to the frame for strength and utility.

The hood is one of the bad points of the De Soto. It is of a shallow design which has very little inherent rigidity and this weakness is not counteracted by sufficient internal bracing. The first notable effect of this fault is the difficulty encountered in closing the hood. Gentle closing will not catch and rough handling causes mismating of the catch. If the hood ornament is used for a handle, the hood begins to buckle. This whole situation is accentuated by the lack of any sound deadener under the hood.

In the gas mileage department the De Soto Firesweep stands up well with

its competition. Its overall town and country average of 12.9 mpg is neither out of line nor at the front of the parade.

The barograph speedometer was quite accurate. At 30 mph it was on the nose; at 45 mph the speed was actually 44.5 and at 60 mph indicated the fifth wheel registered 57 mph.

Acceleration times left a bit to be desired. It went from zero to 30 mph in 4.1 seconds, to 45 mph in 7.2 seconds and to 60 mph in 10.8 seconds.

Considering its size the De Soto is quite light. With its wheelbase of 122 inches, overall length of 216.5 inches and width of 78.3 inches it carries 3900 pounds. The front wheels hold 2230 pounds while the rear wheels account for 1670 pounds. This total weight figure is at least three or four hundred pounds lighter than that of comparable cars from other manufacturers.

Pound for pound the De Soto carries no more nor no less than what is called for in its particular competitive race. Its individual assets are styling moderation in interpreting the Forward Look and happy handling which makes friends easily. ●

Test Data

Test Car: 1958 De Soto Firesweep Sportsman
Body Type: two-door hardtop
Basic Price: $2889
Engine: ohv V-8
Carburetion: single two-barrel
Displacement: 350 cubic inches
Bore & Stroke: 4.06 x 3.38
Compression Ratio: 10-to-1
Horsepower: 280 @ 4600 rpm
Horsepower per cubic inch: .80
Torque: 380 lb.-ft. @ 2400 rpm
Test Weight: 3900 lbs. without driver
Weight Distribution: 57% of weight on front wheels
Power-Weight Ratio: 13.93 lbs. per horsepower
Transmission: TorqueFlite
Rear Axle Ratio: 3.15
Steering: 3.5 turns lock-to-lock
Dimensions: Wheelbase 122 inches, overall length 216.5, width 78.3, height 56.8, tread 60.9 front, 59.8 rear
Suspension: Torsion bars front and semi-elliptic rear
Tires: Tubeless 8.00 x 14
Gas Mileage: 12.9 mpg average
Speedometer Error: Indicated 30, 45 and 60 mph are actual 30, 44.5 and 57 mph respectively
Acceleration: 0-30 mph in 4.1 seconds, 0-45 in 7.2 seconds and 0-60 in 10.8 seconds

BAROGRAPH speedometer is canted to prevent annoying back reflections and to allow speed-checking by the other passengers.

ECONOMY engine of DeSoto line, Firesweep is equipped with a single two-barrel carburetor. Other series have four-barrels.

DE SOTO'S CLEAN LINES MAKE IT ONE OF THE BEST SPOKESMEN OF THE FORWARD LOOK.

Tucked under this DeSoto's hood are enough horses and inches to give it a lively load of "go." With style and fuel economy to boot, the Firedome is a sleek, middle-price performer.

SPEED AGE tests the

By LEN PROKINE & JOE PETROVEC

ASIDE from the fact that it is our job to do so, we run these tests for three reasons: First, we enjoy doing them. Second, we hope you enjoy reading them. And third, the man has not yet been built who can tell exactly what a car will do without taking it on the road. As an example, we offer the '58 De Soto. Falling as it does right in the center of the Chrysler line, with Imperial and Chrysler above, and Dodge and Plymouth below, its performance, theoretically, should fall in the median range between. It doesn't. Our test car carried a single two-barrel carburetor, something of a rarity these days, so it should have had a touch of the weak sister. It didn't. But we'll get to that in due time.

Torsion bars notwithstanding, the Firedome tilts on cornering. Handling, however, is great, with light, responsive
steering. Rear suspension is conventional leaf-spring and
reaction of tail end is conventional on corners. Carrying a
lone two-barrel carb, car showed maximum speed and performance with relatively good economy. Top speed was 114.

DE SOTO

Physically, the De Soto is a beauty, perhaps the best-designed of a gener-ally handsome line. The rear fenders rise gracefully, as a natural conse-quence of the entire design. They are neither tacked on nor built up. From the rear, the De Soto is elegant, clean, sweeping and uncluttered. The grille remains a bit busy and bulky, and there are those six tail-lights, but otherwise the car is perfectly expressed. And the Sportsman body style is the best example of this expression.

From within, our Sportsman was equally clean, almost austere. It was finished in textured fabric and vinyl leather, with side panels of anodized aluminum. Despite the excellence of its design, though, it lacked the look of

real luxury. And this brings us to a common failing of Chrysler's hardtops. In their search for true automotive beauty, Chrysler has been building its cars lower and lower, longer and longer, and the effect is as aesthetically pleasing as all get-out. But when you subtract the considerable length of the hood, the enormous overhang of the rear fenders, the dashing rake of the windshield and the rear window, you're left with what is actually a small pas-senger compartment. With the front seat moved back to give a fairly tall driver leg room, the rear-seat passen-gers are obliged to assume the rough general position of Rodin's "Thinker."

Further, in a low car, there just isn't room for thick cushions and deep up-

holstery. Sports cars and the small for-eign cars solve the problem by substi-tuting support for softness. A well-designed bucket-seat can be every bit as comfortable as an overstuffed chair. But four bucket seats would be lost in a car the size of our De Soto, so it must be offered as a six-passenger ma-chine. As a result, ours simply had thin, flat cushions, and after two hours be-hind the wheel, we wanted to stand up. All Chrysler's experimental ma-chines point to the eventual adoption of the bucket-seat in some form, but the time is not yet.

The dash carried a full complement of round-faced instruments below a straight-line speedometer. These in-cluded fuel gauge, ammeter, tempera-

Trunk of Firedome has plenty of room, most of it running forward. Depth is 65 inches. Finish is rough, but satisfactory.

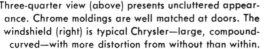

Three-quarter view (above) presents uncluttered appearance. Chrome moldings are well matched at doors. The windshield (right) is typical Chrysler—large, compound-curved—with more distortion from without than within.

ture gauge, and oil-pressure gauge. The arrangement was particularly neat. Heating, ventilation, and defrosting were controlled by a single sliding lever below the dash, and by two switches on the dash. This was a pleasure. It generally takes more skill to heat the modern car than it does to drive it. One thing that puzzled us about the controls was the wheel. It's designed to be gripped below the center, at about 8:20, and this is not the best driving position. Plymouth's engineers know this. Don't they speak to De Soto?

Under the hood, there were 361 cubic inches of displacement, 295 horses, and one two-barrel carburetor. Let's face it—that's an awful lot of stew from a very small pot. We were flabbergasted to see it, and we credit this small gas meter for the 13 mpg figure we posted through hard driving. If we may be permitted to go off on a slight

tangent, we'd like to observe that 13 miles to a gallon is not great, but this was hard driving. And if we invent an index called Miles Per Gallon Per Horsepower, no economy car can match it.

Finally, we come to performance. When we took delivery on our test car at the garage, the gentleman who checked us out on it drove it seven floors down a winding ramp to street level. He made it so fast we thought he would screw us into the basement. When we took over, we found the secret of his success, or part of it. The De Soto steers phenomenally well. The steering booster was the only power assist on our test car, and it produced a lightness and responsiveness that was something to behold. Present power steering units take so much of the work out of steering that it is often difficult to distinguish between them, but this

combination of steering and suspension had a controllability all its own. Without a certain amount of restraint, and some fairly good weight distribution, we could have spread the car all over the road.

Straightway speeds were great for one two-throat carburetor, but a little light for nearly 300 horses. The 0-30 span used up 3.5 seconds, 0-60 took 10.5. Punching the buttons on the TorqueFlite transmission selector did us no appreciable good, which would indicate that the selector mechanism knew what was best under the conditions. We found that in first gear, the car would flat out at about 57 indicated. With the number 2 button depressed, it would shift up at about 72. In Dr, the change-up points were 25 and 55. The standing quarter gave us a best time of 17.3, with an indicated speed of 83 at the conclusion. The

Engine has a single two-barrel carb. Most of mill is readily accessible for servicing, but the plugs are buried beneath exhaust manifolds.

Control panel houses complete set of practical gauges. Heating, ventilating switches are simple and efficient.

Firedome's interior is plain, straightforward, handsome—finished in textured fabric, vinyl leather. Seats are thin, offer insufficient support for long-stretch driving.

flying quarter was under the wheels for 7.9 seconds, for a top speed of 114. This led us to believe that regardless of the car's rated horsepower, a little more breathing and carburetion would have improved its performance greatly. But up would go gas consumption.

We found no shortcomings in the visibility from the driver's seat. These cars are all glass, and we've come to take their excellent road view pretty much for granted. We were surprised, though, to find a great deal of brake fade toward the end of our acceleration runs. We had come to take the excellence of Chrysler's braking systems pretty much for granted, too, and we were disappointed in our test car for pulling up lame. We were also disappointed in the construction of the car. The front end felt a little loose, and we took more shock through the steering column than we like to find.

The torsion bar front suspension gave us a reasonably smooth, firm ride, but it did not do enough to kill dip on braking. Still, it held well enough to keep us from fishtailing or jacknifing around those bends made effortless by the steering. The transmission was good, but it lacked the complete smoothness we had noticed on similar units fitted to other Chrysler cars.

Not only is the De Soto the middle puppy in the Chrysler litter, but our test car, the Firedome, represents the middle range of the De Soto line (Firesweep, Firedome, Fireflite). There is the limited-production Adventurer above the Fireflite, but our test car was pretty centrally placed. It made a respectable showing, with good road manners, beautiful appearance, and all the performance consonant with reasonable economy, but it wasn't in the middle. ●

SPECIFICATIONS:

ENGINE & CHASSIS

CYLINDERS	8
ARRANGEMENT	V-90°
BORE	4.125 IN.
STROKE	3.375 IN.
DISPLACEMENT	361 CU. IN.
COMPRESSION RATIO	10:1
MAXIMUM OUTPUT (HP @ RPM)	295 @ 4600
VALVES	OVERHEAD
CARBURETION	SINGLE TWO-BARREL
TRANSMISSION	TORQUE CONVERTER

OVERALL RATIOS

DR	3.15
2	4.57
1	7.72
REAR AXLE RATIO	3.15
TURNING DIAMETER	49'4"
STEERING	POWER, RACK AND SECTOR
STEERING WHEEL TURNS.. (LOCK TO LOCK)	3.5
TIRE SIZE	8.50 x 14
BRAKE LINING AREA	251 SQ. IN.
SUSPENSION: (FRONT)	TORSION BAR
(REAR)	LONGITUDINAL LEAF
WEIGHT (CURB)	4030
FUEL TANK CAPACITY	23 GALS.

DIMENSIONS

WHEEL BASE	126.0 INCHES
TREAD (FRONT)	60.9 INCHES
TREAD (REAR)	59.8 INCHES
OVERALL LENGTH	218.6 INCHES
OVERALL WIDTH	78.3 INCHES
OVERALL HEIGHT	57.1 INCHES
GROUND CLEARANCE	5.5 INCHES

PERFORMANCE FACTORS

ACCELERATION THRU GEARS	
0-30 MPH	3.5 SECONDS
0-40 MPH	5.3 SECONDS
0-50 MPH	7.5 SECONDS
0-60 MPH	10.8 SECONDS
STANDING ¼ MILE	17.3 SECONDS
SPEED AT END OF ¼	83 IND. MPH
MAXIMUM TIMED SPEED	113.9 MPH

SPEEDOMETER ERROR IN MPH

INDICATED	TIMED
30	32.5
40	41.2
50	50.5
60	58.0

MAXIMUM TORQUE (LBS/FT)	390 @ 2800 RPM
HP PER CU. IN.	.817
LBS. PER HP	13.7
MILEAGE (HARD DRIVING)	13.0

The DE SOTO Diplomat V8

with PowerFlite transmission

DURING our road test of the De Soto Diplomat V8 we covered more than 400 miles, and much of this motoring was done on wet roads.

A clear idea of the safety in which this very large and powerful car is capable of transporting its driver and passengers is provided by the fact that we were able without qualm to time its acceleration from a standstill up to 100 m.p.h. on a very wet surface.

The "Torsion-aire" suspension system, which employs torsion-bar springs at the front and long leaf springs at the rear, performs excellently. It provides a very high standard of riding comfort over all kinds of surfaces, resists roll well when curves are taken fast, and prevents any nose or rear-end "dip" from occurring under the influences of normal braking and acceleration. There is surprisingly little tendency for the rear wheels to spin when hearty acceleration is used on a loose or wet surface.

Low build and a wide track—the latter being exploited to the full at the rear by mounting the springs outboard of the chassis—undoubtedly aid the suspension system to produce the excellent results that it does.

Directional stability at speeds between 80 and 100 m.p.h. is outstanding. The Diplomat's very good road manners are uncommonly little affected by strong crosswinds when it is travelling as fast as 100 m.p.h. (The 5,210 c.c. V8 engine is capable of propelling the car at more than 100 m.p.h., but we do not possess facilities for timing the vehicles that we test at speeds higher than 100 m.p.h.)

It was impossible for us to determine to what extent the Diplomat's prominent tail fins are responsible for its remarkably good straight-line running at high speeds. We *were* tempted to amputate them so that we could make comparative tests—but we felt that, had we done so, it might have been difficult for us to explain our action to the car's rightful owners when the time came for us to return it to them. All we can say is that the fins are there—and so, too, are the advantages that their protagonists claim to result from their presence.

The engine is beautifully smooth and quiet. The Diplomat V8 has abundant power; it will accelerate from a standing start to 90 m.p.h. in 29.5 seconds on a wet road. Like other very powerful cars, its potential is always greater than the requirements of the moment—it needs to be driven with mature judgment and discretion. Light steering, PowerFlite transmission system (torque converter, with push-button selection of range) and power-brakes render the physical effort of driving negligible : the driver has every opportunity of concentrating on "reading" the road and following the course and selecting the speed that best match prevailing conditions and probable developments.

Used at well-chosen moments, the great accelerative ability of the car makes overtaking an unusually rapid and clear-cut, and therefore safe, operation : the opportunity is seen, the accelerator pedal is depressed a suitable extent, and the manoeuvre is swiftly accomplished. With the "D" button of the PowerFlite range-selector pushed in (the condition in which all normal driving is carried out), full depression of the accelerator pedal at speeds below about 60 m.p.h. causes an immediate change-down to be made; ample acceleration is available above about 45 m.p.h. without using this "kick-down", but the extra surge can be valuable in an emergency.

With the "D" button pushed in, there is an automatic change-down when road speed falls to about 11 m.p.h.; the change-up occurs at between about 15 and 60 m.p.h., according to the manner in which the car is being driven. The automatic changes are smoothly accomplished, passengers being rarely aware of them.

When the "Low" button is pushed in no change-up can take place; this is for employment when ascending or descending really steep mountain passes.

As a safety measure, the starter circuit is not completed unless the "N" (neutral) button is depressed. Thus, all the "gear changing" that the driver is called upon to do under usual conditions is to depress the "N" button before turning the ignition key fully to the right to start the engine, and then to depress the "D" button.

There is, of course, also a button marked "R" to look after reversing requirements.

The power-brakes merit praise. They enable this heavy car (dry weight 3,790 lbs.) to be decelerated smoothly and rapidly from 100 m.p.h. with light pressure on the brake pedal. A severe test revealed that even harsh treatment that results in the smell of hot linings becoming evident to the car's occupants does not cause the brakes to fade appreciably.

In a test which simulated failure of the brake-servo, we discovered that the car could be brought to a halt from high speed in a reasonable distance by exerting a pressure on the brake pedal that most men could exert fairly easily with one foot and almost any woman could exert by using both feet on the very wide brake pedal.

Another test revealed that the vacuum-reserve of the power-brakes is fully able to provide normal, power-brake, deceleration from 100 m.p.h. to a halt if the engine should suddenly cease to function due to some such event as the low-tension wire to the coil coming adrift when the car was travelling fast.

The running-in process of the test car was completed while it was in our hands. The first few applications of the brakes from really high speeds were accompanied by mild judders (perhaps it would be fairer to call them tremors) at the front; this disappeared as the brake linings became fully bedded-in to their drums. The point is mentioned because we think that buyers of fast, heavy and powerful cars like the Diplomat V8 should know about it and make sure that they "run-in" their brakes as well as their engines : a few fairly rapid stops from high speeds will ensure that, in any subsequent high-speed emergency, the brakes will perform considerably better than they might without this pre-treatment.

Four headlamps provide excellently for safe high-speed motoring on the open road at night.

The baggage boot has an enormous capacity.

The ease with which the Diplomat V8 is handled despite its considerable size is due to the excellent view-out that the driver enjoys, as well as to the driver-aids we have mentioned (torque converter and power-brakes). The extremities, and large areas of the tops, of all four wings are seen from the driving seat. It is easy for a person of almost any size to make himself or herself really comfortable at the controls; the front seat rises as it is brought forward. The rear-view mirror is positioned so that it causes no blind-spot in the driver's forward view. Windscreen washers form a part of the car's standard equipment, and the windscreen wipers sweep a good area; although, being contra-acting, they leave an unswept "V" in the centre of the windscreen, the driver finds that—unless he is seated far back—the off-side wiper provides him with a fully adequate field of view.

Six really large adults can make themselves very comfortable in the Diplomat without there being any suggestion of restriction other than the fact that the centre-front passenger may find the transmission "hump" a little incommoding unless he or she has fairly short legs. The capacity of the baggage boot can fairly be described as enormous.

Obviously, even in this Sputnik-and-Alpha age, interior space cannot be obtained without exterior bulk, and it must be admitted that it is not always easy to find in a city a parking space that matches the Diplomat's dimensions. The Diplomat is, in fact, larger than some of the white squares that are marked out as parking "bays" : when you cannot park all of it, you park what you can and leave it at that—the traffic officials seem to understand.

Lightly tinted glass is used for the wrap-around windscreen and for the rear window. The speedometer consists of a series of oblongs (each representing 5 m.p.h.) that gradually fill-in in red from the bottom as speed increases. The odometer provides readings down to tenths of a mile. The door-locking system enables entry to be gained via either locked front door. The material that is used for the upholstery provides a good grip on clothes—one does not feel the need for arm-rests to prevent one from sliding about the seats under the influences of fast cornering.

Starting was always immediate during our test—even after the car had been parked in the open overnight in very damp air. The engine warms up to its working temperature rapidly after a start from cold (a study of drawings of the power unit reveals that the designers have avoided having an excessive weight of metal around the vital parts).

Instrument-lighting is excellent; the push-buttons of the PowerFlite transmission system are also discreetly but adequately illuminated at night. A reversing light, at the centre of the rear bumper, is a standard fitting; it is automatically lit when the car's lights are being used and the "R" button is depressed.

The hand-brake is easily applied and has good holding power—the latter point is important because it is not possible to leave the car with the transmission locked so that engine compression will provide an extra "parking brake".

Night-driving is rendered uncommonly safe and agreeable by the four headlamps which illuminate the road ahead excellently when they are all in operation ("high"), and give a first-class spread of light across the road when only the outer two are used ("low" or "dipped") without causing dazzle to oncoming traffic.

The quality of detail work—trim and finish—is no more than adequate, certainly not luxurious, in view of the Diplomat's price of £1,399 (at coast). Viewing the

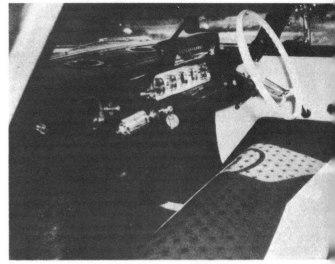

Roominess, comfortable seats, and well-planned controls are among the Diplomat's attractive features.

car on a showroom floor, a prospective buyer might find fault with such things as the quality of the ash-tray and the somewhat drab finish of the facia, but we believe that a test run in a demonstration car would soon persuade him to view these as very minor details against the background of magnificent motoring that the De Soto Diplomat V8 is capable of providing.

Long-distance motoring is an effortless joy in a car such as this. Cruising speed is dictated by road conditions, not by limitations of the vehicle's ability. Hills are flattened out by the surge of power from the engine. Ample space, excellent suspension and very comfortable seats help to ensure that all occupants of the vehicle are relaxed and contented. The driver's mind is made easy by the knowledge that he has but to decide and the car will obey—in particular, he knews that he has but to apply pressure on the accelerator pedal for the car to respond with all the eagerness of Pavlov's dogs answering the dinner bell.

Fairly "quiet" motoring, which, however, included some moderately fast cruising on the open road and some town-driving, resulted in the unexpectedly good overall petrol consumption figure of 21.7 m.p.g. ●

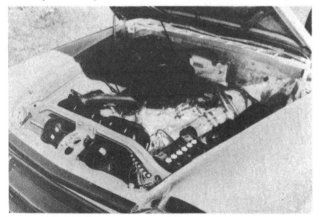

Engine accessibility is reasonably good, although the engine-sump dip-stick is long and tortuous.

SPECIFICATION AND PERFORMANCE

BRIEF SPECIFICATION

Make ... ... DE SOTO
Model ... ... Diplomat V8
Style of Engine V8. Water-cooled. Overhead valves (push-rods operated by single high-mounted camshaft).
Bore ... ... 3·91 ins. (99·3 mm.)
Stroke ... ... 3·31 ins. (84·1 mm.)
Cubic Capacity 318 cu. ins. (5,210 c.c.).
Maximum Horse-Power Approximately 245 b.h.p. (Compression ratio 7·5 to 1)
Brakes Hydraulic. Power-assisted (vacuum servo). Rivetless brake linings.
Front Suspension Torsion bars

(longitudinal). Anti-roll torsion bar.
Rear Suspension Semi-elliptic leaf springs mounted outside frame.
Transmission System PowerFlite automatic transmission — torque converter incorporating two mechanically-obtained ratios. Push-button selection of range.
Overall Length ... 17 ft. 0½ ins.
Overall Width ... 6 ft. 6¼ ins.
Overall Height ... 4 ft. 8½ ins.
Turning Circle Approx. 43½ ft.
Dry Weight ... ... 3,790 lbs.
Price ... £1,399 at Coast Ports
£1,436 in Johannesburg

PERFORMANCE

Acceleration 0-30 m.p.h. 4·1 secs.

0- 40 m.p.h. 5·8 secs.
0- 50 m.p.h. 8·0 secs.
0- 60 m.p.h. 10·8 secs.
0- 70 m.p.h. 15·4 secs.
0- 80 m.p.h. 20·9 secs.
0- 90 m.p.h. 29·5 secs.
0-100 m.p.h. 41·3 secs.
From a steady 40 m.p.h. to 60 m.p.h. 6·5 secs.
From a steady 60 m.p.h. to 80 m.p.h. 11·7 secs.

Maximum Speed Over 100 m.p.h. (see text).
Reasonable Maximum Speed in "Low" ... ... 65 m.p.h.
Fuel Consumption ... 21·7 m.p.g.
Test Conditions Sea level. No wind. Wet road. 90 octane fuel.

Desoto

DE SOTO FOR '59 retains basic Forward Look under detailed changes. Bumper, grille, headlights and tail lights redesigned. New roofline on 4-door hardtops. Interior changes include oval steering wheel, bar-type speedometer. Swivel seats and pushbutton weather controls are available. Other new optionals are self-adjusting (electric eye) rear view mirror, automatic headlight dimmer, air suspension unit. 13 accessories optional last year are now standard on some models . . . . Firesweep, Firedome and Fireflite offer 4-door sedan, 2- and 4-door hardtop, convertible. Firesweep and Fireflite have 4-door wagons (2 or 3 seat). Adventurer has 2-door hardtop,

convertible. Torqueflite is standard on Fireflite, Adventurer; power steering and brakes on Adventurer . . . . Urge output is 290 hp (Firesweep), 305 hp (Firedome), 325 hp (Fireflite), 350 hp (Adventurer). Adventurer engine optional on all models . . . . Price range from cheapest to most expensive is $2900 to $4740 . . . . All models will handle six comfortably (up to nine in wagons). . . . Handling is unchanged, Level-cruise air suspension (optional) with Torsion-aire (standard) will improve ride . . . . Slight displacement increase should mean better performance . . . . Major tune, about $14. Depreciation, about $500 per year.

DE SOTO

Advertised delivery price:
$3366 (Firesweep Shopper) to $4358
(Fireflite Explorer).

THERE ARE four De Soto wagons for '59. The Firesweep 122-inch wheelbase chassis has two four-door models, the six-passenger Shopper and the nine-passenger, three-seat Explorer. The same two models are repeated on the 126-inch wheelbase Fireflite chassis with more luxurious trim.

Interior dimensions are the same on all models, with 119.7 inches from back of front seat to extended tailgate, 33-inch interior height and 62.5-inch-wide load compartment.

Upholstery is extremely comfortable and interior trim is luxurious, especially on Fireflites. Air conditioning is available of course, and on nine-passenger models an additional evaporator unit mounts on the wagon's ceiling between the second seat and the rearward-facing third seat.

In nine-passenger wagons, De Soto solves the spare tire stowage problem by eliminating it in favor of tires with "captive air" inner tubes on all road wheels.

De Soto wagons are extremely comfortable on all types of road surfaces, especially the longer and heavier Fireflite models, which along with the Chrysler New Yorker wagons are the biggest of all U. S. wagons, measuring 220 inches from bumper to bumper. In spite of their size, the De Sotos are quick-turning and easy to maneuver with power steering, providing the space is available.

Firesweep models are equipped with a 290-horsepower version of Chrysler Corporation's newly designed "B" series engine. Fireflites get the 383-cubic-inch-job rated at 305 horsepower. Either engine is more than adequate to roll the heavy wagons fast as anyone could want them to go. ●

KEYNOTE OF DE SOTO'S 1959 FRONT END STYLING IS MASSIVENESS. THE BASIC WEDGE SHAPE HAS BEEN RETAINED AND GREATLY UNDERLINED.

THE 1959 DE SOTO

De Soto, the car that's almost hit the bottom in market penetration, has been given—the stylists insist—a "complete personality change!" Having dropped drastically from 1957 to 1958, worried division chiefs hope that new manufacturing facilities in Detroit plus revamped styling will boost De Soto back up into a bigger sales league.

STYLING

QUESTION is: Is a facelift enough for De Soto's dilemma? Somebody up there seems to think so and some of the negative attitudes are shrinking under the impact of new optimism. It appears this optimism is based more on the uncertainty and hope of what the public will buy—and it *may* buy De Sotos —rather than on the 1959 changes themselves. With a new management at the helm, it could be a switch for the better!

Keynote of De Soto's front end styling is massiveness. The basic wedge shape has been retained and greatly underlined. Almost half of the car's front end consists of a large two-section bumper with a long horizontal air scoop between the lower and upper bumper sections.

A narrow aluminum grille with horizontal lines stretches across the top of the bumper between the headlights. Dual headlights are set lower in the front end (similar to the 1959 Chrysler) and are capped by new front fenders. Apparently the stylists used every front end line to stress width and lowness.

De Soto's newly styled rear end includes a large double-bar rear bumper with aluminum recessed between the two bars of the bumper. Fins sweep upward to form a hood over the triple taillights.

The entire rear end treatment slants forward, making it appear low and in motion. All elements of the De Soto rear end treatment are completely new and yet, the stylists claim, retain distinctive De Soto identification.

Side color sweep treatments for De Soto are new, including a gold anodized aluminum insert for the Adventurer and silver anodized aluminum available for all other De Soto cars.

Rubber-tipped bumper guards are available for the first time for the front and rear bumpers in each series. These are standard on Adventurers and Fireflites.

De Soto has a new four-door hardtop roof with sculptured design and raised rear section for increased headroom. Rear window glass area has been increased 15 per cent on all De Soto four-door hardtops. A new roof treatment on the Adventurer series features black or white simulated leather finish of textured vinyl paint.

The De Soto Firesweep is available in the following six types: two-door hardtop, four-door hardtop, four-door sedan, four-door station wagon (two-seat), four-door station wagon (three-seat), and the convertible. Firedome is available as a two-door hardtop, four-door hardtop, four-door sedan, or convertible.

Six types are available in the Fireflite series: the two-door hardtop, four-door hardtop, four-door sedan, four-door station wagon (two-seat), four-door station wagon (three-seat), and the convertible. The Adventurer can be had either as a two-door hardtop or as a convertible.

Inside the 1959 De Soto, popular convertible styling is used more widely. Pleated vinyl interiors are now available in the Firedome, Fireflite and Firesweep hardtops as well as convertibles.

Vinyl with a newly developed simulated pleat is used in conjunction with standard cloth interiors on Firedome and Fireflite hardtops. The addition of a fourth trim option to the De Soto model insures a better matching of interior and exterior colors than ever before.

A new polyurethane headlining is standard on Adventurers. Rear seat foam rubber padding has been added to the standard equipment of all De Sotos with the exception of Firesweeps.

Instrument panels are new, including a full-width aluminum insert as standard for Fireflite and Adventurer models. A new bar-type safety speedometer is featured and indicates green to 30 miles per hour, yellow from 30 to 50, and red above 50. Instrument panel padding, formerly standard only on Adventurers, is now standard on all models except Firesweep. Also of new design on De Soto cars are steering wheels, wheel covers and all medallions and jewelry.

ENGINEERING

Introduced for the first time on all 1959 Chrysler cars are new push-button heating and air conditioning controls. The simplified push-button controls completely take over the job of adjusting car "climate" including the operation of all damper doors and other elements of the heating or heating and air conditioning systems.

In place of levers or other controls spread along the instrument panel, a series of pushbuttons—arranged horizontally on the right side of the instrument panel—are easily reached and marked "Off," "Low," "Def," and "Vent."

Along with the remarkable simplicity of operation and ease of control are a number of engineering improvements which make these heaters and air conditioners quite unique.

These include: A divided air duct below the instrument panel to direct air simultaneously to both sides of the car and along the floor; newly-designed air distribution outlets mounted on top of the panel. These consist of two lowered grilles which can be rotated by the driver so as to direct air to any area of the car. The grilles are no longer flush with the top of the panel as in former models, but project slightly above the surface. The new units also provide a 10 per cent increase in air conditioning capacity.

Standard engine for all Firesweeps is a 361-cubic-inch V-8 with 10.1 compression ratio. It has a bore of 4.12 and a stroke of 3.38 inches. A two-barrel carburetor is standard with dual exhausts standard on convertibles and optional on other cars.

The engine for the De Soto Firedome is larger with a displacement of 383-cubic-inches, a compression ratio of 10.1-to-1, a bore of 4.25 and stroke of 3.38 inches. A two-barrel carburetor is standard on this engine and dual exhaust is standard on convertibles, optional on other models.

Fireflite uses the same engine as the Firedome with identical compression ratio and bore and stroke. However, it does utilize a four-barrel carburetor. Dual exhaust is standard on convertibles and optional on other Fireflites.

The hottest engine of the lot is used in the De Soto Adventurer, but it is also available as an option on the other cars. The Adventurer engine has a displacement of 383-cubic-inches, a compression ratio of 10.1-to-1 and a bore of 4.25 and stroke of 3.38 inches. However, this power plant uses two four-barrel carburetors, dual exhaust, special camshaft, distributor, air cleaners, valve springs and damper. It definitely produces more power than the standard V-8's!

Approximately 100,000 De Sotos were produced at the Detroit factory in 1957. But, it is estimated in some quarters that they may be producing much less than that amount in all of 1958! Most agree, however, that things should be looking up for '59. ●

NEWLY STYLED REAR end includes a large double-bar rear bumper with aluminum recessed between two bars of bumper. Fins sweep forward, form a hood over triple taillights.

NEW SIDE COLOR sweep treatments for De Soto include a gold anodized aluminum insert for the Adventurer and silver anodized aluminum available for all other De Soto cars.

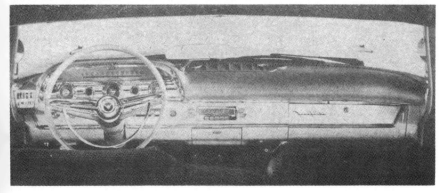

FULL-WIDTH aluminum insert highlights the all-new instrument panel. Panel padding is now standard on all models but Firesweep.

EXCELLENT roadability and a high degree of riding comfort are two outstanding De Soto characteristics again in 1959—as they have been, in fact, for several years.

Add increased responsiveness offered by larger engines, a greater degree of styling change than was made for 1958, several detail mechanical improvements, some totally new features and you have what De Soto hopes is a line of products capable of winning back some of the sales lost during the 1958 model year.

Judging from the Fireflite hardtop tested for this report, De Soto has grounds for optimism.

One factor that undoubtedly hurt De Soto during the past year was that only a very minor facelift was made in changing over from 1957 to 1958.

Perhaps this wouldn't have hurt so much if the industry-wide recession—which hit the medium price field especially hard—hadn't occurred. At any rate, De Soto decided to take no chances and made more extensive styling changes for 1959 than long range plans called for originally.

The result is 1959 models, while still bearing a basic resemblance to the first Forward Look cars of two years ago, have been altered enough in appearance so they won't easily be mistaken for 1957 or 1958 cars.

Another factor which certainly hurt De Soto and all other Chrysler corporation cars during 1958 was the generally poor

reputation for quality earned by the company's 1957 models.

This was extremely unfortunate in view of the otherwise high standards of the automobiles and because the vast majority of defects were more annoying than serious.

Steps to correct this situation were taken during 1958 and efforts have been intensified for the new model year. If the Fireflite tested is any criterion, the quality upgrading program has been successful in several important areas.

One of these is improved sealing against water leaks, a weak point in a number of Chrysler-built automobiles tested in the past.

The Fireflite test car went through a veritable cloudburst without a drop of water leaking into the passenger compartment or trunk. Several trips through auto washes also failed to produce any leakage.

Less body shake was apparent on rough roads than has been true of most Chrysler products in the past two years. Other points generally indicative of care in assembly included trim moldings that lined up properly, no loose or misplaced weather stripping and a minimum of ripples in sheet metal panels.

As far as overall on-the-road performance is concerned, the test car was at least equal to other makes in its class in most respects and distinctly better than average in many.

Roadability and ride have been mentioned as excellent and there is no other way to put it. For as large a car as the Fireflite is, it does a terrific job of imparting a feeling of handling confidence to its driver.

Nor does the fact that it has slightly higher spring rates at

DE SOTO ROAD TEST

Roadability, riding comfort and acceleration give De Soto optimism for '59

LARGE-DISPLACEMENT V-8 engine (383 cubic inches), sensible rear axle ratio, good three-speed automatic transmission give De Soto excellent acceleration through all usable speed ranges.

its wheels than some competitive makes penalize occupants in terms of comfort, since the suspension definitely is a long way from being firm or harsh.

(In fact, other suspension engineers could well profit from De Soto's example. There has been a tendency to go slightly overboard in the direction of ultra-soft springs in the last two years. After a certain point returns in ride smoothness seem to diminish and controllability is sacrificed without a compensating improvement in comfort. Another case of "if a little is good, more is not necessarily better!"

Performance was another Fireflite strong point. The combination of a large-displacement V-8 and sensible rear axle ratio coupled by a very good three-speed automatic transmission resulted in very good acceleration through all usable ranges.

Two criticisms leveled at 1957-58 De Sotos, particularly

SPACIOUS TRUNK is quite adequate. Newly styled rear, slanting forward, includes large double-bar bumper and triple taillights.

Test Car: 1959 De Soto Fireflite
Body Type: four-door hardtop
Basic Price: $3888
Engine: ohv V-8
Carburetion: single four-barrel
Displacement: 383 cubic inches
Bore & Stroke: 4.25x3.38 inches
Compression Ratio: 10.1-to-1
Horsepower: 325 @ 4600 rpm
Horsepower per cubic inch: .85
Torque: 425 @ 2800 rpm
Test Weight: 4300 lbs.
Weight Distribution: 2279 lbs. (53%) on front wheels
Power-Weight Ratio: 13.23 lbs. per hp
Transmission: TorqueFlite three-speed automatic with torque converter
Rear Axle Ratio: 3.31-to-1
Steering: 3.5 turns lock-to-lock
Dimensions: overall length 221.1 inches, wheelbase 126, width 78.7, height 55, tread 60.9 front and 59.8 rear
Tires: 8.50x14
Gas Mileage: 13.2 overall average
Speedometer Error: indicated 30, 45 and 60 mph are actual 31, 45 and 59.5
Acceleration: 0-30 in 3.5 seconds, 0-45 in 5.6 and 0-60 in 8.9

INSTRUMENT PANEL features padding, newly designed steering wheel. Location of inside mirror is same as '58 but electronic dimmer for night travel is new.

DE SOTO FIREFLITE TURNED IN EXCELLENT ROADABILITY, HIGH DEGREE OF RIDING COMFORT AND SHOWED OVERALL QUALITY IN ROAD TEST.

hardtops, have been difficult entry and exit and inadequate headroom in rear seats.

The first problem is partially solved in 1959 by optional swivel seats—with which the test car was equipped. There are some who will feel these offer more theoretical than practical advantages, but they certainly do have some value to those who will make it a habit to use them.

(It's possible that they would be more useful if spring-loaded lightly so they would return to normal straight-ahead position after driver and/or passengers got out, however.)

Rear headroom has been increased slightly, but even a reasonably tall man still will have trouble wearing a hat back there; same thing is true in the front seat.

Despite the impressive width of De Soto seats, the test car was most comfortable with only four adults aboard. A middle passenger in the front seat definitely would not enjoy a long ride. The situation is not so bad for a middle passenger in the rear seat, but he certainly won't be as comfortable as those riding on each side of him.

Placement of the inside rear view mirror on all Forward Look cars has been a bone of contention since 1957. There have been consistent complaints that they created a blind spot to the right front of the car—which could be especially annoying in some right turn or parking situations.

The problem was less in the test car as the mirror standard projected out of the side of the instrument cluster housing and barely projected above the top of the padded dash. Forward visibility was virtually unimpeded.

This low placement cut low-angle vision directly behind the car somewhat, but an excellent sideview mirror controlled from inside the car made this of no great importance.

In short, De Soto for 1959 has a lot to recommend it. The styling changes aren't revolutionary but are more obvious—though not necessarily better—than those made for 1958. The excellent ride, handling and performance should help offset any advantages of competitive makes with more radical appearance changes. And, very important, if quality can be kept to the same standards exhibited in the Fireflite tested, there should be no reason this Chrysler division can't improve sales substantially over the dismal 1958 showing. ●

Fireflite two-door hardtop has new unit construction under its graceful styling. Massive, "300" type grille dominates front.

CAR LIFE

CONSUMER ANALYSIS

DE SOTO was the first of the new 1960 Chrysler Corporation cars that I test drove, so I run some risk of being prejudiced in its favor. It was behind the wheel of a '60 DeSoto hardtop on Chrysler's vast proving grounds in Chelsea, Michigan—a veritable "little America" of different roads—that I first experienced the triple-threat of the refined Torsion Aire suspension, the all-new unit body and frame construction, and the most thorough vibration and sound insulation job in the industry.

This combination of solid, shakeproof body and fantastically comfortable ride matched with equally impressive handling and a vibrationless, nearly soundproof engine operation makes an automotive "package" that's hard to beat and hard to resist.

Yes, DeSoto has an excellent engine too, but for this year the car's performance in (*continued on page* 76)

de soto: definitely different for '60

By JIM WHIPPLE

respect to ride, roadability and bank vault solidity was so exciting to me that I didn't care whether there was a 200 or 300 horsepower engine under the hood.

As a matter of fact there are two DeSoto V-8s for 1960. The standard powerplant of Fireflite models is a 361 cubic inch engine developing 295 horsepower. Optional engine on Fireflites is a 383 cubic inch job with four barrel carburetor developing 325 horsepower. Standard engine on Adventurer models is a 383 cubic inch powerplant with a two-barrel carburetor rated at 305 horsepower.

As an optional engine on Adventurer models DeSoto offers the 383 engine with fabulous new Ram Charge manifold consisting of two four barrel carbs mounted out above the valve covers of each bank of four cylinders. Each four barrel carburetor feeds the intake valves of the opposite bank of cylinders through manifold tubes approximately 30 inches long.

At medium engine speeds these tubes create harmonic waves in the incoming stream of fuel-air mixture in such a way that at the moment of intake valve opening the mixture has a greater velocity, consequently, more mixture surges into the combustion chamber than would be the case with conventional manifolding.

With no increase in displacement or raising of compression ratio Ram Charge manifolding adds 25 horsepower and 50 lbs ft or torque to the 383 engine over its ratings with a single two barrel carb.

In this case the horsepower isn't as significant as the torque, which is a measure of actual engine thrust or turning power. The additional torque afforded by Ram Charge comes in at about 2800 rpm and boosts take-off and passing power. According to engineers at Chrysler Corporation Ram Charge doesn't cut into engine economy at around-town speeds.

But no matter what engine option may be fitted to the '60 De Soto you won't be able to feel it, and in all but 3/4 to full throttle operation you won't notice the sound of it either. Principal reason for the delightful silence is a painstakingly thorough job of sound engineering. Engineers crawled all over the car's interior with sensitive electronic "listening devices," finding the sources of resonance and the primary pathways of noise from the road and engine to the passenger compartment. Then came careful applications of different absorbing and deadening materials. Result, De Soto is a truly quiet car and a veritable paradise for napping kids and back seat snoozers.

While on the subject of De Soto's comfort, it's worthwhile to mention that the new "Unibody" structure is virtually free from the rubbery quiver and shake which has so often characterized the road feel of separate body and frame cars. At the same time, De Soto's unit body does not have the weird periodic vibrations and mysterious drumming that sometimes crop up in improperly engineered or constructed unit body jobs.

De Sotos have completely new bodies, with every steel stamping in the body and frame being new for 1960. As a result the engineers had a chance to make some very sizeable improvements in the usable space of the passenger compartment and the convenience of entry and exit as well as in driver vision.

Basically, these improvements are a result of the switch to unit body-frame construction eliminating the space-robbing duplication of chassis-frame plus body-frame and the vertical space taken up by body mountings. As a result the '60 De Soto has become a genuinely roomy car with comfortable seat heights and 44 inches of legroom in the rear seat of sedans.

What the figures don't tell you is that the depressed rear floor areas are wide and the tunnel is less obtrusive, and that the center of the rear seats is once more a comfortable seating position. The size of the transmission hump has been reduced so that the center passenger in the front seat is more comfortable.

Not only are the '60 De Sotos comfortable to sit and ride in but easier to get in and out of as well. Door frame openings are an inch or so higher, the slight "dogleg" at the windshield corner post has disappeared and the rear door openings are wider and more handily laid out. Swivel seats are optional on all models and for this year are linked with the door by concealed cable, so that now they swing out when the door opens.

Although De Soto bodies are roomier than last year's, they have the same basic dimensions as the '60 Chryslers. Wheelbase has been reduced to 122 inches on all models, in place of last year's 122 for just the Firesweep and 126 for the top two series. This move, plus the consolidation into two lines—Fireflite and Adventurer with four door sedan and two and four-door hardtop models—is an effort on the part of Chrysler top management to find a unique place for De Soto.

In years past De Soto tried to compete in three different price fields, lower, middle and upper medium-price. In other words they were attempting to compete with Dodge via the short wheelbase Firesweep, and with Chrysler Saratogas and New Yorkers with the big Fireflite. For 1960 De Soto has its own spot in the lineup—it has a Chrysler sized body on Dodge's 122 inch wheelbase. Result—a more compact and maneuverable luxury car.

The proven formula of front torsion bars and assymetrical leaf springs combined with Oriflow shock absorbers that Chrysler Corporation dubbed Torsion Aire remains essentially the same as in 1959—with a slight but significant exception. Spring action on small rapid bumps like cobblestones has been softened by easing up on shock absorber control. De Soto suspension engineers were able to do this because of the vastly superior rigidity of the Unibody construction, which successfully resists tendencies for rapid oscillation of suspension parts, i.e. shake.

Power steering is pretty nearly a must, as it gives you the advantage of a quicker ratio, which permits you to maneuver the fairly large and hefty car with deftness and precision in heavy traffic or on winding roads.

To sum it up, the '60 De Soto is a roomy, solidly built car with an unbeatable combination of comfortable ride, road hugging stability, and easy yet precise control. It has a low sleek silhouette into which extremely clever engineering has designed a spacious and practical compartment for six passengers and plenty of luggage. De Soto hits its target as a car with close to the maneuverability of the low priced three and nearly the luxury and silken behavior of the highest priced cars.

FROM AIRFLOW TO ADVENTURER....

BY JIM WHIPPLE

FOR most of its life DeSoto has been a leadership car. Even when it was introduced, 'way back in 1929, it was at the head of its field in design and engineering with steel bodies, hydraulic brakes and a high compression six-cylinder engine. Shortly thereafter came synchromesh transmission and, in 1934, the big step, DeSoto's Airflow.

Because of its introduction in the depths of the depression and because it was an utterly new conception, with an understandably startling new appearance, it never inspired the public and thus never got off to a solid start commercially.

It did however inspire just about every team of design engineers in Detroit, because the Airflow provided many of the basic principles of today's cars. Although it looks hopelessly out of date standing side-by-side with a low, sleek '60 Adventurer, let's take a look under the paint and see how much of its heritage today's DeSoto owes to the remarkable Airflow.

At the time Airflow was produced other cars of the day were little changed in basic design principles from the cars produced before World War I. Their frames were virtually straight beams that allowed the bodies to twist and rattle as the wheels passed over irregularities in the road. The passenger compartment was placed at the extreme rear of the car. Most of the space in the comfortable center of the chassis was occupied by radiator, engine and transmission, while rear-seat passengers sat crowded between the rear wheels and, as they sat high up in the air and directly over the axle they were bounced and swayed about. (*continued on page* 79)

A '60 DeSoto wheels through a sharp turn with little or no roll.

Set for a trip to the past is car tester Jim Whipple who grins in amazement from behind the wheel of '34 Airflow with its truly "dark ages" visibility, above. The "space age" arrives with the easy—to—enter '60 DeSoto below, with its immense areas of glass.

Author Whipple points to box section frame-body sill member, one of the structural strongpoints of the rock solid '34 DeSoto's unit body.

Not the Black Hole of Calcutta but the "fully enclosed" luggage compartment of the '34 Airflow, above, which makes a startling contrast to the immense, easy to reach trunk of a '60 DeSoto.

Simple, sturdy and not too powerful was the 1934 Airflow DeSoto engine, above, tester Whipple found it creditably quiet and vibration free, 1960 DeSoto V-8, below, is rated at four times the power of the Airflow Six.

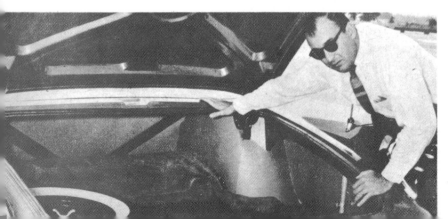

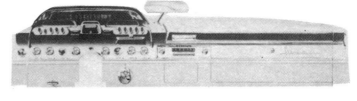

Neat, complete and fairly readable is the instrument and control set up on Airflow's panel. Night lighting is much superior on hooded cluster of instruments on '60 DeSoto.

DeSoto's Airflow came upon the scene like a breath of fresh air in a damp cave. First of all the passenger seats were moved forward so that the rear seat was no longer cramped between the wheel housings nor perched uncomfortably over the rear axle. Secondly, the engine and transmission were moved forward so that the radiator and a portion of the engine block were located over, and even in front of, the front axle.

As a result of this redistribution of weight, the load on front and rear springs became more nearly equal so that rear springs could become a good deal softer in action while front springs could be firmed up to carry the heavier and more stable front end while the degree of spring reaction, or "ride rate," could be coordinated between front and rear to give a slower, more comfortable body oscillation in responses to a given road bump. This was one of the biggest breakthroughs in suspension engineering since the invention of the shock absorber.

Thirdly, the body was widened at the cowl and front doors so that the front seat could actually accommodate three people. Granted neither Airflows front or rear seats were as wide or as comfortable as seats today . . . but in the frame of reference of 1934 the Airflow was the first car in America where six passengers could be accommodated comfortably on just two seats.

But, unnoticed by the crowd was DeSoto's integral body and frame structure . . . the first of its kind to be produced in America and the direct forerunner of the amazingly quiet, solid Unibody of the 1960 DeSoto.

DeSoto engineers gave me the unique opportunity of driving a '34 Airflow DeSoto four door sedan and a 1960 Adventurer four door hardtop in the same afternoon. The impact of a full quarter century of design and engineering progress could be seen and felt in the space of minutes.

The sturdy old Airflow was in very good condition. It had been privately owned and had some 34,000 miles on the odometer. No effort at rebuilding or restoration had taken place and little was needed. I was particularly impressed with the quality of the paint—original black—

and the workmanship on the interior trim and upholstery.

In comparison to the '60 Adventurer on the road the Airflow seemed absurdly high almost like a truck. The thick windshield corner and door posts made for intolerable blind spots compared to the broad expanse of glass and sweep of vision in the '60 Adventurer.

The Airflow ride was incredibly full of little jounces and jiggles, and the high-riding car seemed to lean if I even thought about turning a corner. In one respect however, the old Airflow measured up all the way through a quarter century of advancement. Its integral, welded body and frame was just as resistant to shake and rattle as the 1960 Adventurer! And that means well nigh perfect. But after ten minutes at the wheel of the old Airflow I realized just how much DeSoto has done for the American motorists in 25 years.

The biggest advances, and for my money the most important ones, have come in the area of ride, roadability, ease of control and safety as embodied by DeSoto's Torsion-aire suspension system, its excellent power steering and its smooth-acting Total Contact brakes.

Next on the list of improvements would be the latest version of Forward Look body design with excellent all around vision and comfortable seating positions. After that, I think I'd put the smooth-shifting Torque Flite automatic transmission with its new and accessible push buttons, followed by DeSoto's powerful and efficient V-8 engine.

What other advances are left? Literally hundreds; everything from washable, durable synthetic upholstery fabrics and foam rubber cushioning to DeSoto's "deep dip" rustproofing

What of the future? Just as the old Airflow established the pattern that others followed, so will the competitors hasten to embody the advancements of today's DeSoto in their cars of next year or the year after. Meanwhile DeSoto engineers will be back at those drawing boards working at even greater engineering and design breakthroughs that will put tomorrow's DeSoto still further ahead and make it a still better car.

THE NEW DE SOTO MAKES NO BONES about being a big, luxurious car, one of the most powerful ever constructed." So starts an announcement ad for the '60 DeSoto. It goes on to say that it ". . . gives you the steadiest, quietest and safest ride—bar none!" and that it ". . . offers every kind of luxury option: Thru-way Auto-pilot, *automatic* swivel seats, Ultra-Fi phonograph—the *works!*"

It sure *is* big, lacking only eight inches of being as long as a Cadillac 62; it *is* luxurious in feel and *is* powerful, if **not** ". . . one of the most powerful ever constructed." It will get up off its haunches and amble down a straightaway about as fast as any stock '60 Detroit dragster. It lacks only tenths of seconds of being as fast as its brother-under-the-skin, the Dodge Dart D-500, one of the fastest "accelerators" of the year.

Comparing those figures on the opposite page to a Dart with ram induction, the DeSoto Adventurer comes off second best by slight margins: for instance, it gets to 60 mph from a dead standstill only 0.3-second slower than a Dart and gets through the quarter-mile trap doing 85.5 mph (vs. 86) in 17.2 secs. (vs. 16.3). That's pretty good for a bigger, heavier car that uses the same 330-hp rated engine.

You can expect lots of response from a ram-inducted engine, particularly in mid-speed ranges. These twin-carbureted engines have lots of torque throughout a wide rpm range, which is really more of a clue to acceleration than horsepower. At almost any speed you stomp the throttle you'll feel a heavy hand shoving you back in your seat. You can also expect to have some servicing problems, because you won't find it easy to get at the spark plugs, nor will it be simple to check the valves. With lots of underhood units needed to run the optional equipment staring a service station attendant or mechanic in the face, you had better plan on doing some of your own servicing—unless money is no object to you.

What about the ride? It's good for driver and passenger alike, as we found by taking it over straight stretches, then up over 7000 ft. into snow country. On the highway at high speed the car acted fine, though some dips had a tendency to take the steadiness out of its stance; a few times we felt that the front end had a rotating motion, instead of just the normal up-and-down movement that most cars have after they come out of a dip. Around mountainous curves, taken both slow and fast, body lean and the tendency to "break away" were both slight; the contour of the seats helps to keep either driver or passenger from rolling from side to side.

As for some of the luxury items—the Auto-pilot, phonograph and swivel seats—they each have their advantages: the Auto-pilot, if you do lots of driving on thruways where there's little traffic; the phonograph, if you have 45 rpm records and are tired of listening to radio commercials; and, the swivel seats, for their novelty value. Frankly, I fail to see any particular advantage to the seat swiveling out automatically as you push the door open. They are attached together by a cable, but after you sit down on the seat and swing it into its straightforward position, you still have to reach for the door handle to pull the door shut. It would make more sense if the door would *automatically close,* too.

What about the rumor that Chrysler is going to drop the DeSoto? This has flamed up again since Ford has dropped the Edsel: in the latest sales tallies for '59 the two cars are only a few hundred apart, with DeSoto having the lowest total of the Chrysler cars (outside of Imperial). DeSoto officials, nevertheless, say they have no intention of pulling the plug, claiming they have plans for DeSoto cars ". . . up through '62." There are those who say, however, that any new DeSotos planned will be luxury versions of the Valiant. If so, driving around in a '60 Adventurer in a few years could be a rare thing—not too unlike driving a Continental today.

* * *

NO SOLITUDE ON THE SOLITUDE

TRYING TO MAKE GOOD TIME around the six-mile Solitude Circuit, a seldom used, high-speed road course near Stuttgart, Germany, is one thing when the side roads are blocked off. It's strictly another when you have to stab the brakes to avoid hitting a horse-drawn cart, have to jerk the wheel to avoid running over a tractor on the side of the road and when you don't know how much room you have for an unexpected slide in a turn because you may meet another car head-on. Even so, in a Mercedes 220-S —normally considered a family car—I had a ball. It corners fast, has good power, looks modern, is fairly easy on gas and is as comfortable as any car I've ever driven. What more could you ask from a car?
—**Walt Woron**

Acceleration

0-45 mph 5.8 secs.		0-60 8.8
Quarter-mile 17.2 secs., 85.5 mph		
30-50 4.3	45-60 3.0	50-80 8.4

D E SOTO'S overall design is focused on power, performance and responsiveness in a smartly styled automobile which maintains a high level of comfort and convenience. The Adventurer, with the optional ram-induction V-8 powerplant, is a notable example of how well this has been accomplished.

Handling is one of the Adventurer's major attractions and most drivers will like, even prefer, its responsiveness. Sensitive steering is a contributing factor. The car's turning circle is good for its wheelbase and the steering, 3½ turns lock-to-lock, is quick and accurate.

The car is precise in parking and belittles the fact of its bigger size. At any speed correcting for uneven road conditions requires substantially no effort and it is simple to keep the car moving in

a straight line. In city driving the Adventurer will whip in and out of traffic lanes with cat-like agility.

The De Soto executes corners vigorously and its suspension and chassis seemed to be tuned for sharper turning than most drivers will ordinarily encounter. This engineering is probably necessary since the car's quick steering and powerful acceleration will encourage faster cornering. On even the sharpest corners the Adventurer tracks true with no tendency for either end to break away from the circle. Body lean is negligible and there is very little tendency to pitch the passenger or driver to one side although this is due in part to the contour of the seats.

The Adventurer has impressive acceleration and must be classed among the hotter 1960 cars. Throttle response is almost instantaneous and even though the transmission is automatic, torque is relayed to the rear wheels nearly as efficiently as a stick shift. This eager acceleration owes much to the optional 3.31 axle ratio which compensates for the Adventurer's extra weight. Standard is a 2.93 axle which would reduce acceleration and increase the mpg figure somewhat.

This ultra-responsiveness is not lost at traffic speeds and in the low rpm range is actually multiplied. Opening the throttle at any speed hurtles the car forward even quicker than using a passing gear would. At higher speeds the effect is still there although subdued to a degree.

With a powerplant this size there are bound to be some disadvantages. One is economy and the ram induction engine has an acquired craving for fuel. The engine compartment is crowded and several vital components are conspicuously inaccessible. Many service and minor repair jobs will be difficult and time consuming procedures, increasing the labor expense.

These are only minor considerations to some people, however,

and will be discounted against the De Soto's performance record. One thing no true power enthusiast will overlook though is the engine's vocal reaction to power. When the throttle is opened the ram manifold produces a vibrating sound similar to those made by dual exhausts. This resonance is not harsh and grating. Instead, it is a low, throaty rumbling indicative of power.

Roadability in the Adventurer is good both at slower city speeds and faster open highway rates. In the country the De Soto will maintain high speeds without inducing fatigue. The springing seems to be a good compromise which is not too soft to cause objectionable swaying on the open road nor too harsh for comfort in town. On uneven roads practically the only vibration transmitted to passengers is the audible slap of the tires against the pavement.

Entry and exit from the passenger compartment cannot be called good. The Adventurer was equipped with automatic swivel seats and they are a decided advantage when the door can be fully opened. But more often than not, especially when parked near another car, they cannot be used at all.

Inside, the front seat is adequate for only two persons. A third passenger would definitely be cramped and nearly impossible to seat if the car has the optional record player. The Adventurer has a swing down arm rest in the center of the front seat. This device gives the driver good support on long trips. In fact, the front seat is, for all practical purposes, two individual seats with an upholstered arm rest between.

Entry and comfort in the back seat are limited and passengers would find that long trips would be fatiguing. The rear window is large and has unobstructed visibility. To prevent back seat passengers from becoming sunburned this window has an iron oxide coating.

The instrument cluster is a well arranged layout and has good contrast between indicator and dial face permitting easy reading. The speedometer is a sweep hand needle and gives the driver an instant indication of his speed. The whole instrument cluster must be viewed through the steering wheel, however, and this can be disadvantageous varying with individual drivers. Depending upon their height some drivers can not see all the gauges without head movement. The steering wheel rim interferes with the speedometer for some, while others cannot see the gas gauge on the left. A small point, but irritating when driving, since both these gauges are important and must be frequently referred to.

Automatic transmission controls are pushbuttons placed in a straight row to the left of the driver. Their action is simple and positive, practically eliminating any chance for error in shifting. Visually balancing these buttons is another row placed on the right side controlling the heater and fresh air. Push-pull controls are in a horizontal row below these pushbuttons and are handy for the driver.

One accessory, the record player, can be enjoyed by nearly anyone but honestly appreciated by only those who realize the difficulties that had to be overcome before it could become a workable and practical option. Despite vibration, noise and outside interference, the record player works well and plays two hours of standard 45 rpm records with excellent sound reproduction.

De Soto's Adventurer is a remarkable automobile in many ways. It is sporty, yet has tasteful restraint that keeps it from being ostentatious. The Adventurer's engineers have made a wise selection of components and combined them into an automobile which actually gives more than it promises. It handles well enough to be driven by a woman, yet the controls are not mushy and will appeal to men who prefer accurate, positive handling. ●

1960 DE SOTO

TEST CAR: De Soto Adventurer
BODY TYPE: Two-door hardtop
BASE PRICE: $3663

Test Car

Interior Room

SEATING CAPACITY: six
FRONT SEAT—
   HEADROOM: 34.4 inches
   WIDTH: 63 inches
   LEGROOM: 46.2 inches
TRUNK CAPACITY: 29.7 cubic feet

Engine & Drive Train

TYPE: ohv V-8
DISPLACEMENT: 383 cubic inches
BORE & STROKE: 4.25 x 3.38
COMPRESSION RATIO: 10-to-1
CARBURETION: Dual four-barrel with ram manifold
HORSEPOWER: 330@4800 rpm
TORQUE: 460@2800 rpm
TRANSMISSION: three-speed automatic
REAR AXLE RATIO: 3.31

Maneuverability Factors

OVERALL LENGTH: 217 inches
OVERALL WIDTH: 79.4 inches
OVERALL HEIGHT: 54.8 inches
WHEELBASE: 122 inches
TREAD, FRONT / REAR: 61 and 59.7 inches
TEST WEIGHT: 4355 lbs.
STEERING: 3.5 turn lock-to-lock
TURNING CIRCLE: 43.7 feet curb-to-curb
GROUND CLEARANCE: 5.2 inches

Performance

GAS MILEAGE: 10 to 15 mpg
ACCELERATION: 0-30 mph in 3.9 seconds,
  0.45 mph in 5.7 seconds and
  0-60 mph in 8.8 seconds
SPEEDOMETER ERROR: indicated 30, 45 and 60 are
  actual 32, 47 and 61 mph respectively
POWER-WEIGHT RATIO: 13.2 lbs. per horsepower
HORSEPOWER PER CUBIC INCH: .86

ONE OF THE HOTTER CARS of 1960, the ram-induced De Soto V-8 is extremely responsive in the low and middle rpm ranges. The throaty rumble of the ram tubes is the most exciting sound Detroit has yet uttered. But this power gimmick has definite drawbacks, primarily in the fields of economy and engine servicing. Other points are covered fully in this test report of the Adventurer.

• DESOTO

The '61 DeSoto features complete restyling and important mechanical changes

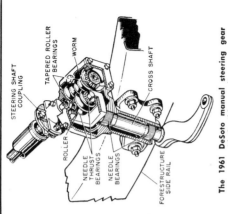

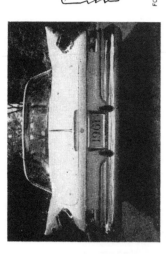

The 1961 DeSoto. Two-door and four-door hardtops are only models offered this year.

DESOTO has trimmed its body types for 1961 to two-door and four-door hardtops. There are no sedans, convertibles or station wagons.

Fins similar to those of 1960 have been retained, but otherwise styling is completely changed. Head lamps are canted, and a screened airscoop extends horizontally above the grille, which is a horizontal bar type. The front bumper sweeps upwards at the ends, in keeping with the canted headlamp design. Wraparound tail lights are placed lower in

the fin ends than in 1960. The back window extends well up into the roof line, and the windshield now runs straight up to the roof without the former high-forehead curvature at the top.

The power plant is a 361-cu.in. V8, in which the compression ratio has been reduced from 10.0:1 to 9.0:1 for more efficient operation on regular grade fuel. Equipped with a single two-barrel carburetor, this engine develops 265 hp, and there are no engine options. Intake valve diameter is increased to pro-

vide efficiency equal to the higher compression engine used in 1960. Torqueflite automatic transmission is standard.

DeSoto shares several mechanical changes with other Chrysler lines. These include the new Chrysler-built distributor with nylon breaker arm pivot and rubbing block, solenoid starter shift to engage starter gear, and rubber-tipped needle valves in the carburetor float chamber to eliminate flooding. DeSoto also has a pull-out-push-down parking brake release and a fabric universal joint in the steering shaft to reduce vibration. An AC

alternator has replaced the DC generator for better current output at low engine speeds.

The instrument panel continues the same cockpit design as in 1960, with all instruments grouped in front of the driver in tiers for good visibility.

As in other Chrysler lines, the body is unitized construction, and the torsion bar suspension in front with leaf springs in the rear is continued.

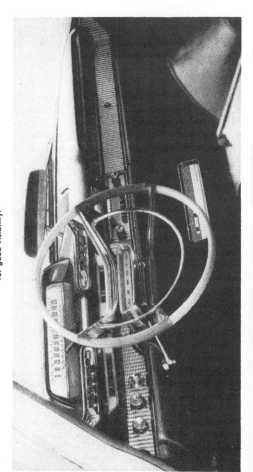

The 1961 DeSoto manual steering gear with flexible coupling.

The DeSoto rear end. Wraparound tail lights are placed lower in the fin ends than in 1960.

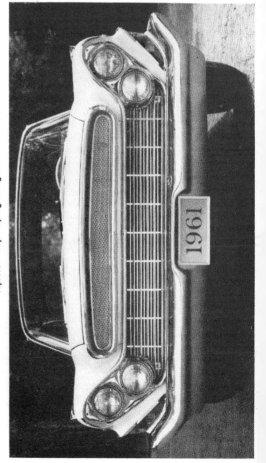

The DeSoto instrument panel. Instruments are grouped in front of the driver in tiers for good visibility.

The 1961 DeSoto front end. Canted head lamps and upswept bumper ends represent major styling changes.

DE SOTO'S major styling change is a new two-section grille and canted headlights.

1961 line-up offers one series, two body styles and one engine

De Soto

FULL-WIDTH chrome-trimmed aluminum grille blends with canted headlights. Screen pattern covers functional engine airscoop.

RIBBON-TYPE speedometer is in separate hooded case on top of cowl. Pushbuttons control automatic transmission, air, heater.

1961 DE SOTO

Engines

Cubic Inches	Type	Compression Ratio	Carburetors	Torque	Horsepower
361	V-8	9.0:1	2-bbl.	265	370

Dimensions Compared (in inches)

Car		Wheelbase	Length	Height	Width	Front Tread	Rear Tread
1961	De Soto	122.0	215.4	54.8	79.4	61.0	59.7
1960	De Soto	122.0	215.4	55.0	79.4	61.0	59.7

WHAT HAS HAPPENED to De Soto this year is exactly what has happened to many other medium-priced lines. Body styles are sharply reduced in number, styling changes are not extensive, there is greater emphasis on economy and only one engine is available.

De Soto's styling changes are not extensive, rather they are more of a facelift. The most pronounced difference is in front where a full-width grille of horizontal aluminum strips contrasts with a chrome molding. At either end of the grille, the canted dual headlights are encased with a die-cast molding which carries the grille outward and upward.

Above this grille is the De Soto's most distinguishing treatment—a functional airscoop spanning the full width of the hood. The scoop has a screen pattern and is outlined with a bright molding, with the De Soto name in block letters of gold on chrome spaced across the metal mesh.

Fins are somewhat similar to the 1960 model but have been restyled to give them model year identity. Instead of fairing into the front door, the new fins begin with a reverse curve and sweep quickly upward to a point at the rear.

There is no series designation this year and all 1961 De Sotos will be called simply, a De Soto. Choice of body styles has been reduced from the six last year in two series to only two—a two-door and a four-door hardtop.

De Soto will have only a single engine this year with no options available. Gone from the line-up is last year's 383-cubic-inch powerplant with its three performance options.

This year the emphasis is on economy and the engine is the powerplant that was standard for the Fireflite series last year. Engine displacement remains unchanged at 361 cubic inches but the compression ratio has been reduced from 10 to 9.0-to-1 to enable the De Soto to use regular gasoline. The engine uses a two-barrel carburetor.

One engineering development is rather important although a major reason for its adoption is because it is a Chrysler-produced unit. This is the all-new manual transmission which will be standard equipment on both models. It features a 2.55-to-1 low gear ratio, a 1.49-to-1 second gear and 3.34-to-1 reverse gear. All gears are helical for quiet operation. Second and third are synchronized for smooth shifting, and involute splines on the main shaft reduce gear backlash. The transmission case, clutch housing and transmission extension are made of cast iron.

Other improvements include an AC alternator (instead of a DC generator), a power steering pump that is self-adjusting for belt tension as increased pump torque requires, easier operating and more conveniently located parking brake pedal, and safer brake release lever. ●

De Soto's most significant new identifying feature is the front, where a distinctive airscoop spans the full width of the hood.

ALL 1961 DE SOTOS ARE HARDTOPS. DE SOTO MAINTAINS ITS STREAMLINED APPEARANCE OF MOTION WITH SWEEPING FINS.

MANY OBSERVERS seriously doubted whether De Soto would introduce any car, let alone a new car for 1961. Generally speaking, most persons thought that if the car did come out, it would be a luxury compact. De Soto does have a new car this year but it shows typical evidence of what is happening to medium-priced luxury cars. The line is reduced in body styles from six to two, series designation has been dropped and all engine options are gone. Moreover, De Soto's standard engine will burn regular fuel. What developments there are, are refinements and innovations which are shared with every other Chrysler Corporation car.

De Soto's styling this year is basically a facelift. Its most significant identifying feature is in front, where a distinctive airscoop spans the full width of the hood. On the rear deck are five sculptured lines, an identifying styling gimmick first used on the 1957 Adventurer.

Only two body styles, a two- and a four-door hardtop, will be available. There will be no series designation this year and all cars will be called De Soto.

The 361-cubic-inch V-8 engine that is standard in both De Sotos has a 9-to-1 compression ratio. The ratio has been lowered from 10 to permit the engine to operate on a lower-octane fuel rating. Performance should be relatively unaffected, however, because the intake valves have been enlarged for greater efficiency.

Outside of the lower compression ratio this powerplant is relatively unchanged from last year. There are two refinements in the carburetor. A rubber-tipped needle valve in the float bowl makes the unit less sensitive to flooding by enveloping small dirt particles and still maintaining a good sealing against the needle seat. The second feature is a two-stage step-up jet. This device provides better fuel flow at cruising speeds.

Another engine innovation De Soto shares not only with all Chrysler cars but in some form with all Detroit cars that will be sold in California. This is a closed crankcase ventilating system that is being installed to reduce smog-producing hydrocarbons.

The closed system will replace the conventional system ordinarily used on other cars. It consists of a special carburetor, a spring-loaded valve and a flexible tube connecting the valve and carburetor. The carburetor has a special calibration and contains a fitting just below the throttle blades into which the crankcase vapors are drawn by suction. From here they pass into the intake manifold where they are burned.

The new Chrysler-produced manual transmission will be standard on all cars. Optional will be the Torqueflite three-speed transmission that was available last year. The alternator

and distributor, that are also Chrysler-built, will be standard equipment in the electrical system.

Another area where modifications have been made is in the steering system. Manual units now have a fabric-reinforced rubber coupling between the steering gear and shaft plus new needle bearings. The power steering pump has an ingenious arrangement which permits it to tighten the belt according to the pump drive torque requirement. As the torque load increases the belt becomes tighter, improving efficiency. When the load is small, only the weight of the pump rests against the belt, which results in longer life for the belt.

Other improvements in De Soto include new materials to be used in the interior fabrics and floor covering and refinements in the speedometer, under-hood silencing pad, shock absorbers, parking brake and rust-proofing techniques.   /MT

fewer body styles and an engine designed for lower octane fuel

■ Stylistically, the Adventurer II is a unique blending of American and European motifs. The jet-exhaust tail lights are a distinctly American feature, while the body proportions and roofline are decidedly European.

OR A CAR called the Adventurer II, this swoopy, extravagant, one-of-a-kind Mopar Hemi-powered *granturismo* has spent an awful lot of its existence in the garage. Like Paul Henreid and Ingrid Bergman, the Adventurer II was once stranded in Casablanca—not at Rick's *Café Américain* awaiting letters of transit, but at the local Chrysler dealer waiting for a buyer. The hapless De Soto spent three lonely years in a showroom before a U.S. Air Force employee rescued it, shipped it back home, and then sold it to a Floridian builder-developer who subsequently stored it for nearly three decades.

It seems this is one Adventurer that only rarely sees the light of day. But this is getting ahead of our story. . . .

That story began in 1949, when then-40-year-old designer Virgil M. Exner left Studebaker for the top position in Chrysler's advanced styling studio. Exner's aversion to the gaudy, bloated look of postwar Detroit is well documented. "Today's car," he told the American Society of Body Engineers in 1948, "has become so heavy and bulbous that it appears to have been fashioned at the forge of Vulcan rather than in the design studios and fast-moving production lines of ingenious American industry." But "Ex" never had a bad word to say about Italian automobile design, which he described to the Society of Automotive Engineers in a 1951 address as "thoroughly modern, with subtly rounded shapes and sharp accents indicative of genuine character," and to *Car Life* magazine readers in October 1954 as "a happy blend of modern smoothness with the classicism of a day long past . . . best of all, the Italian

DE SOTO ADVENTURER

HERE'S LOOKING AT YOU, KID

car *looks* like an automobile."

Even before Exner's arrival, both Pinin Farina and Ghia had built one-off sedans on Chrysler Corporation's chassis. Exner was not particularly impressed by the styling of Ghia's Plymouth-based XX-500, but its flawless workmanship and modest $10,000 cost convinced him that Ghia could build styling prototypes for Chrysler's Advanced studio. This Ghia did, beginning with the very continental Chrysler K-310 in 1951, followed by the C-200 and SS in 1952 and the d'Elegance in early 1953. Then

Chrysler management decided to give the other divisions a turn, so the 1953 Firebomb and Firearrow series were all labeled Dodges, while the *original* Adventurer was badged a De Soto when it made its debut in November 1953.

Most of these now-famous show cars were designed by Exner who, with Cliff Voss and Maury Baldwin, produced everything from sketches to final ⅜-scale clay. The plaster models were then shipped from Highland Park to Turin, where Ghia's craftsmen translated them *by eye* into full-size steel bodies.

BUT THE Adventurer II arrived by a different—and somewhat more circuitous—route. In 1953, Ghia crafted a sleek and stunning coupe body for aircraft engineer Virgilio Conrero's tube-frame, Alfa Romeo-powered entry in that year's Mille Miglia. Rife with rocketship shapes and cues, its futuristic form was created by Ghia engineer Giovanni Savonuzzi, who had previously conceived the Cisitalia sports-racer that became the Abarth 204-A. The Conrero fared poorly in competition, but Ghia unveiled virtually identical coachwork for the Fiat 8V chassis at the 1953 Paris salon. Fiat agreed to a limited production run of 50 cars.

Early in 1954, Ghia design chief (and majority shareholder) Luigi "Gigi" Segre brought pictures of the Alfa-Conrero to Detroit to show to Exner. "It was a beautiful design," recalls Exner's son, Virgil, Jr. "That Alfa really grabbed us." Paul Farrago, a Detroit-area race-car builder who sometimes served as Exner's Italian translator, bought one of the Ghia-bodied 8V Fiats, so Ex had a chance to examine the shape up close and in the metal. Then Segre suggested an adaptation of the same styling theme as a follow-up to the De Soto Adventurer. Ex enthusiastically agreed, pledging his support and Chrysler's money. Ghia completed the De Soto Adventurer II in time for it to pose for pictures at the dedication of Chrysler's new Chelsea Proving Ground in the spring.

Ex, Jr says that his father exerted "a little bit of influence" on the final form of the Adventurer II, "to make it a Chrysler car rather than a purely Italian car." But he allows that "Savonuzzi had more to do with it than anyone else." *Motor Trend* disparaged the Adventurer II in August 1954, suggesting that its "slab sides and the illusion of excessive width violate the Exner trademark, which is emphasis on the mechanical beauty and function of an automobile." In fact, the Adventurer II rather pleased Exner, as his son recalls: "He certainly approved of it, even if it wasn't exactly what his next phase was going to be.... That was when my father realized that Savonuzzi was not only a great engineer but had a terrific styling eye."

Despite its racy sheet metal, however, the Adventurer II was a competent but hardly stunning performer. Built on a standard De Soto Series S-19 chassis with a 125.5-in. wheelbase, it was powered by a smaller version of the Chrysler Firepower hemi displacing a modest 276 cu in. and developing 170 bhp with 7.5:1 compression. Its 2-speed PowerFlite automatic transmission and "full-time" power steering were new De Soto features in 1954. The latter, according to De Soto publicity, did "80 percent of the work of turning and parking." Contemporary testers said it eliminated 100 percent of the road feel. But it did allow a relatively quick ratio, only 3¼ turns lock-to-lock.

In August 1954 *Road & Track* published photos of the Adventurer II on Ghia's stand at the Turin auto show. After that, a bit of haze settles over the car's history. Its first documented private owner was Art Spanjian, a U.S. civilian who made his living at Nouasseur Air Base in Morocco. In 1959, Spanjian told *Automobile Topics* that the Chrysler agency in Casablanca had purchased the Adventurer II at an auction following the auto show in Brussels. The dealer had hoped to sell the car to Morocco's King Mohammed, but after merely borrowing it for a week, Mohammed handed back the keys and declined to sign on the dotted line.

Spanjian wanted the car, but didn't want to pay the $25,000 that the dealer figured he needed to cover his investment so far. Art haggled over the price for three years, until the Air Force appointed him chief of Maintenance Planning—in Dayton, Ohio. With his bags already packed, Spanjian made one last offer for the Adventurer. He didn't tell *Automobile Topics* how much. He revealed only that it was more than $2500, less than $10,000—and that the dealer accepted it.

Unfortunately, Art didn't say much about the precise timing of these events, which makes it difficult today to confirm or deny the reality of the royal test drive. Sultan Sidi Mohammed ben Yusuf was progressive, pro-Western and popular with his people—but not with Morocco's French colonial rulers, who forced him into exile in the summer of 1953. In his place the French installed his elderly uncle Mulay Arafa, whom they regarded as more compliant—but whom the Moroccan citizens regarded as generally useless. An armed revolt in 1955 convinced the French to allow the Sultan to return to his loyal subjects that autumn and to proclaim himself King Mohammed V, a title he

The engine-turned instrument panel brightens the interior.

retained until his death in 1961. Exactly when Mohammed (or perhaps Mulay?) found time amid this turmoil to toy with a new red sports car, I cannot say for certain.

■

THE ADVENTURER II surfaced again in the showroom of a Chrysler-Plymouth dealer in Dayton, Ohio, probably in 1960. Armand Archer, Sr, a Fort Lauderdale developer, was visiting his family in Dayton for the Christmas holidays when he bought the Adventurer as a present for himself on December 26. He remembers only that its previous owner (who was in the showroom at the time) "was with the State Department" and was "practically in tears" because he had been transferred back to Morocco and couldn't take the car with him. He could not recall if this man was Art Spanjian—but it seems unlikely that it was anyone else.

Archer drove the Adventurer back to Florida (averaging a respectable 21 mpg) but soon found that owning a genuine show car can be

91

more frustrating than fun. Curious crowds were always a problem, and irreparable damage a possibility. "It had no bumpers," Archer said, "and the grille was made out of 5000 pieces of individually extruded aluminum." Discouraged, Archer locked the Adventurer in a friend's garage, where it remained for 26 years.

Armand Archer, Jr, a Corvette enthusiast himself, retrieved the Adventurer in the fall of 1986, dusted it off and offered it for sale—still with less than 15,000 original miles on it. Collector Ken Behring snapped it up about two years later and restored it in time for the 1989 Pebble Beach Concours. Today, the Adventurer II crouches in Behring's Blackhawk museum, as cherry-red and perfect as it appeared on Ghia's show stand in Turin 36 years ago. Once again, though, it probably won't be seeing much adventure . . . at least not for a while. ■

De Soto
Adventurer II

SPECIFICATIONS

Price	na
Curb weight, lb	na
Wheelbase, in.	125.5
Track, f/r	56.3/59.6
Length	214.2
Width	77.9
Height	55.5
Fuel capacity, U.S. gal.	17.0

ENGINE & DRIVETRAIN

Engine	ohv V-8
Bore x stroke, mm	92.1 x 84.9
Displacement, cc	4525
Compression ratio	7.5:1
Bhp @ rpm, SAE net	170 @ 4400
Torque @ rpm, lb-ft	255 @ 2000
Carburetion	1 Carter 2-bbl
Transmission	2-sp automatic
Final-drive ratio	na

CHASSIS & BODY

Layout	front engine/rear drive
Brake system, f/r	12-in.-dia drums
Wheels, f/r	15-in. dia
Tires	7.60 x 15
Steering type	na
Suspension, f/r:	unequal-length A-arms, coil springs, tube shocks/ live axle, semi-elliptic leaf springs, tube shocks

PERFORMANCE

0–60 mph, sec	na
Top speed, mph	na

na means information is not available.